# James Logan's "The Duties of Man As They May Be Deduced from Nature"

NOT ADDED BY
UNIVERSITY OF MICHIGAN LIBRARY

NOT ADDED BY
UNIVERSITY OF MICHIGAN LIBRARY

# James Logan's "The Duties of Man As They May Be Deduced from Nature"

## An Analysis of the Unpublished Manuscript

Norman Fiering

American Philosophical Society Press
Philadelphia

Transactions of the
American Philosophical Society
Held at Philadelphia
for Promoting Useful Knowledge
Volume 111, Part 3

Cover Photo: Portrait of Logan by Thomas Sully, 1831, in the collection of the Library Company of Philadelphia. The painting is a copy commissioned by the Library Company after a fire destroyed a portrait from life. Sully based his image of Logan on a painting from life by Gustavus Hesselius in the possession of the family. The Hesselius portrait now belongs to the Historical Society of Pennsylvania. Credit: The Library Company of Philadelphia.

Copyright © 2022 by the American Philosophical Society for its Transactions series.

All rights reserved.

ISBN: 978-1-60618-111-9
Ebook ISBN: 978-1-60618-116-4
U.S. ISSN: 0065-9746

**Library of Congress Cataloging-in-Publication Data**

Names: Fiering, Norman, author.
Title: James Logan's "The duties of man as they may be deduced from nature"
  : an analysis of the unpublished manuscript / Norman Fiering.
Description: Philadelphia : American Philosophical Society Press, 2022. |
  Series: Transactions of the American Philosophical Society Held at
  Philadelphia for Promoting Useful Knowledge ; Volume 111, Part 3 | "U.S.
  ISSN: 0065-9746"
Identifiers: LCCN 2022024921 | ISBN 9781606181119 (paperback) | ISBN
  9781606181164 (epub)
Subjects: LCSH: Logan, James, 1674-1751. | Ethics--United States--Early
  works to 1800. | Ethics--United States--History. | Philosophy,
  American--18th century. |
  Merchants--Pennsylvania--Philadelphia--Biography. | United
  States--Intellectual life--18th century. | Philadelphia
  (Pa.)--Biography.
Classification: LCC BJ354.L64 F44 2022 | DDC 172--dc23/eng/20220802
LC record available at https://lccn.loc.gov/2022024921

# Table of Contents

# Prologue: The Moral Order from Hobbes to Hutcheson

In the two hundred years from 1600 to 1800 the foundations of the moral order in the West altered dramatically. Not only was the overt appeal to theology as a supportive structure largely abandoned, with mundane principles like utilitarianism substituted instead, but the rich Classical tradition of Aristotle and Cicero was also left behind in many respects. Of course, no historical change is total. There are always continuities—old wine in new bottles, terminological novelties that are lacking in real substance—but even with these qualifications there can be no doubt that certain elements from the past were permanently discarded, and potentialities of human society and human nature were emphasized that formerly had hardly been recognized, let alone nourished to realization.

Historical accounts of these two centuries of revolutionary change in Western mentality do not always depict the exact nature of the re-founding of moral values. There are useful concepts, such as secularization or enlightenment, that seem to serve well enough for describing the unraveling or disintegration of the old rationales, but the philosophical enterprise of rebuilding, of creating in ostensibly naturalistic terms a new synthesis, is usually left imprecise. We are prone to feature in this period the revolutions in cosmological theory, in mechanics, and in the mathematics of physical science, a series of developments that certainly did reshape the Western world-view, but the scientific revolution is not the same as the revolution in the foundations of ethics, although there were important connections between the two. It is also necessary to keep the strictly philosophical crisis distinct from such fundamental matters as social, political, and economic change, and changes in mores and customs. The philosophical crisis raised questions concerning the basis of moral obligation, the rational justification of absolute codes of right and wrong, and the propensities of human nature—abstract questions, but urgent, nonetheless.

We must begin with an attempt to sketch out the foundation of morals as it stood before the seventeenth-century upheavals, looking for common principles that more or less united Protestants and Catholics, Stoics and Peripatetics, nominalists and realists, Augustinians and Aristotelians. We find, first of all, the nearly universal conviction that the entire creation has been ordered in accordance with divine reason, that man among corporeal creatures is the closest to God because of his possession of a rational soul, and that reason is man's leading faculty and the natural master of his conduct. Man is also, by virtue of his rational nature, inherently a moral creature, in the sense that he cannot escape thinking in moral categories or judging in terms of right and wrong. He finds himself also unavoidably under the conviction of guilt when he has transgressed. This moral awareness was presumed to be present in pagans, or gentiles, through the principles of natural law, which exist as part of human consciousness itself. Every man has what St. Jerome called the spark of conscience, or synteresis, which included in later medieval elaborations both the elementary general principles of justice and fairness and the reflexivity, or self-consciousness, that brings the self to judgment when the laws of nature are breached.

The impressive moral understanding and performance of some of the ancient pagans, represented supremely in either the lives or the writings of eminent figures like Socrates, Plato, Aristotle, Cicero, and Seneca, were to be understood as no more than an enhancement of the principles of natural law without divine assistance. But it was also widely believed and taught that the Pre-Socratics and even Plato had in fact borrowed certain fundamental ideas from Judaic revelation, perhaps via Egypt, which thereafter informed all Classical philosophy.

The Bible had two important functions in the older moral tradition. Not only did it reveal uniquely the highest moral law, including secrets undiscoverable to the natural mind, such as the principles of Christian charity, but it also, at the same time, confirmed as authoritative and final all that it presented. The latter function was in some respects more important than the substantive revelations. The pagan philosophical schools, for all their ingenuity and even profundity, were mired in the problem of relativism; an elevated ethic like the Stoic competed on perfectly equal terms with the preachings of the Epicureans. Christian revelation, then, brought order to the moral chaos of the ancient world, providing standards by which that which was worthy could be recognized and appreciated.

Nevertheless, the educational tradition of the West—one might even say, the traditions of civilization itself, of arts and sciences, of culture—was Greco-Roman, with the result that from the beginning of the universities, the teaching of moral philosophy was largely bifurcated. There were, in practice, two moral orders, the natural and the supernatural. All university education in ethics, including that at tiny Harvard College in the seventeenth century, on the fringes of European civilization, was based on Aristotle's Nicomachean Ethics, which taught that human nature was adequate for the achievement of human ends, namely happiness on earth through activity in accordance with virtue. Meanwhile, however, in the teaching of divinity or in any Christian exercise, men were told that human nature of itself was inadequate for the attainment of the highest end, eternal salvation, for which divine assistance is needed.

Aside from this division in ends or purposes—happiness on earth in the pagan mode versus eternal happiness—there was also the long-standing argument that Classical ethics was essentially behavioral, that is, directed toward external activity only. Aristotle advocated magnanimity and liberality, but he did not trouble himself to any degree with regard to the intentions or motives of the agent. Christian ethics, on the other hand, was directed toward internal renovation, toward regeneration and the re-orientation of the spirit, toward overcoming concupiscence, which was the prideful and inordinate vaunting of self in disregard of the higher claims of spirit and law. Despite the difficulties presented by this accommodation, the two approaches to ethics were mostly accepted as being complementary in university teaching.

The entire moral structure, both supernatural and natural, inner and outer, was upheld by a social and political consensus, which was expressed in the administration of law and justice; but it was sustained above all by the sanctions of the afterlife. The retributive providence of God might not always be apparent on earth, often the wicked prosper and the good suffer, yet all would be set right in the end. Fear of eternal punishment in hell and the hope of reward in heaven were a constant reinforcement to virtue and morality, even though the Stoics and many Christian writers regarded conduct that was influenced solely by the mercenary passions of fear and hope to be only minimally meritorious.

Much more could be added to delineate further the framework of the moral universe of, say, 1600, but the main elements of the structure have been touched on. In 1624, for example, Lord Herbert of Cherbury listed the five notitiae communes (common notions) that all men must consent to, and indeed do naturally consent to by instinct if they are to be considered fully human: (1) that there is a supreme deity; (2) that He ought to be worshipped; (3) that the worship of God requires above all virtuous and pious conduct; (4) that vices and crimes must be expiated by repentance; and (5) that there is reward and punishment after this life. These famous innate tenets, often looked upon as the earliest expression of deism and thus an anticipation of the future, may also be taken as a summary of some of the core principles of morality as it was established in the West. Lord Herbert tells us something about the past as well as the future. Tenets 2 and 3, that God ought to be worshipped and that worship includes virtuous conduct, establish the ground of moral obligation. Number 4, the necessity of repentance, implies both that man knows innately the difference between good and evil and that he is free to choose the good. Number 5, concerning the afterlife, also implies that man is a free agent justly held responsible for his actions. We should add to this list, also, the widespread assumption that morality is grounded in reason as well as in divine will.

All that I have introduced thus far may be summarized in a few phrases: a deity with rational attributes, who is identified with Truth, Beauty, and Goodness, and has rational expectations of man; synteresis and conscience, which unites man with divine law; freedom and responsibility; providential reward and punishment.

The disintegration of the philosophical synthesis depicted here was brought about by numerous causes on many different levels of human activity, as one would expect. We know that ideas like materialism and atheism, or subversive parties like libertines and freethinkers, did not suddenly originate in the seventeenth century; so, the problem is that of discovering why the revival of Epicureanism, of ancient atomism, or of cults with nihilistic tendencies suddenly found receptive audiences among intellectuals, or suddenly seemed alarming to the faithful. The history of ideas alone, however, is insufficient to explain the sudden currency of previously ignored or suppressed forms of thought. Here I can merely describe.

Whatever the case, the disconcerting and ultimately disintegrative ideas came from many sources, not all of which were intentionally subversive of the received moral tradition. There were, for example, potent anti-intellectual, or better, anti-rationalist forces in the Protestant Reformation, men who were willing to vest all in the motions of the Spirit, without regard to rational criteria of judgment. One might look at antinomianism as only one exorbitant facet of the widespread pietistic movement of the seventeenth century that despised the Classical inheritance and the moral philosophy that came with it. Luther for one, and many subsequent Protestants, passionately rejected Aristotle's ethics as a distraction from the main duty of life, which was attaining salvation through Christ. The bifurcation referred to earlier between external civil duties and internal reform was deliberately undermined as being artificial, and, worse, false, since Christian precepts covered all of life. The "practical-theology" movement, exemplified in the writings of the English Puritan divine William Ames, who was immensely influential in seventeenth-century New England, attempted to remove the philosophical study of ethics from university training, reserving all for divinity or theology. Throughout the seventeenth century the expansion of theology was an object of contention at Harvard. The issue, ultimately, was whether moral theory based on natural knowledge alone could have anything to offer to a regenerated Christian.

If religious movements like pietism and fideism were at least potentially disabling to the philosophical synthesis upon which Western moral beliefs stood, even more damaging was the attack from the other side, that is, from radical naturalism, which would deny the validity of any alleged supernatural revelation and of the transcendent authority of conscience. Equally antithetical to the received tradition was metaphysical materialism, mechanistic thinking that placed man in a concatenation of physical causes such that notions of freedom and responsibility became meaningless. The rational endowment of human beings was, in this theory, only incidental to moral conduct rather than being an essential element in it. Reason was neither a determinant of ends (that is, of goods, of that which is desirable in itself) nor an essential ingredient in the process of free moral choice. Human moral conduct was believed to be analyzable in the same terms as the behavior of animals. Related to these ideas was an ethical relativism that denied the existence of absolute standards of conduct. All of these reductive notions were found either expressly or implicitly in the writing of Hobbes, among others. By 1677, when Spinoza died, nearly all of the presumptions of the old moral structure had been astutely and challengingly questioned: the moral efficacy and authority of divine reason and will, the existence of an afterlife of reward and punishment, human moral autonomy, a transcendent natural law binding on men, the immutability of good and evil.

From this state of disarray came the reformulation of moral philosophy and the emergence of what may be called "the new moral philosophy," a middle-stage in the twenty-five-hundred-year history of the subject when, for a time, it was believed that through an analysis of man himself as a purposeful animal, and of human relations, a complete, authoritative ethics could be derived. Leaving aside pagan antecedents, one may think of three stages in the history of ethics as follows: the medieval stage, when moral philosophy was controlled by the churches and by theological considerations that often were enlightening but also sometimes distorting; the stage of the "new moral philosophy," or the humanistic stage, running from about 1650 to 1850; and the stage that began in the middle of the nineteenth century when essentially sub-human criteria—biology or chemistry, or the unconscious—or particular aspects of human activity, such as the marketplace—were widely used as the basis for ethical theory. In the middle stage, the beginnings of which we are looking at here, the drawing of analogies to the natural world, the world of physics primarily, was a great stimulus to fresh thought. In fact, this analogizing to nature is one of the characteristics of the new moral philosophy that distinguishes it from the prior stage. The third stage was also naturalistic, but in this later case the analogy is not to a teleological vision of the Creation. Instead, the belief prevails that man is implanted in a world less than himself at his best, since it is a world lacking in intelligence, and that no ethics can be true for him that neglects that lesser world.

Not all of the ingredients that made up the reformulation of ethical theory were truly discontinuous with the ethical preconceptions that came before, but many were. Terms like nature, experience, self-evidence, moral sense and sentiment, fitness and suitability, benevolence, utility, and sympathy, and methods like intuition, introspection, rational demonstration in the geometrical mode, and the analogy to nature, come immediately to mind as characteristic of the new era. The roots of the seventeenth- and eighteenth-century reformulation, of course, run deep—one could dig down almost indefinitely and find antecedents in Erasmus or Grotius, in Abelard or Bonaventure, in Augustine or Origen, and so on back to the ancient pagans—but it does not do too much damage to the facts to begin with some of the writings in the seventeenth century where it is already evident that something organically new has coalesced. Leaving aside, then, many perfectly valid claims concerning antecedents and anticipations in earlier writers, I have been most impressed in my own reading by the originality and fecundity, and by the pervasive influence, of two works: Richard Cumberland's *De Legibus Naturae*, first published in Latin in England in 1672 and translated into English in 1727, and Nicolas Malebranche's *Recherche de la Vérité*, first published in French in 1674–1675 and translated into English twice, both in the year 1694. From Cumberland and Malebranche one can move smoothly to Henry More and then to the third Earl of Shaftesbury and Samuel Clarke, who, with opposing views, were the recognized leaders of British moral thought at the turn of the century.

Cumberland was a churchman, ultimately Bishop of Peterborough, but there is no evidence this vocation inhibited the philosophic imagination he brought into play against the egoistic view of human nature and against ethical relativism. He expressly rejected appeals to the authority of divine revelation and to innate ideas, like the theory of synteresis, and set about to answer Hobbes by drawing only on "sense and daily experience," on self-evident propositions, and on what seemed to him to be demonstration as rigorous as that used in mathematics. Like every important thinker in the second half of the seventeenth century, he was tremendously impressed by Descartes's achievements in mathematics and natural philosophy and saw in Descartes's principles the possibility of powerful reinforcements for the defense of the inherited absolute morality. "I have illustrated my Subject with Comparisons . . . taken from Mathematicks," Cumberland wrote (he could have added mechanics, too), "because they, with whom I dispute [namely, Hobbes], reject almost all other Sciences." "It seemed worthwhile to shew," he continued, "That the Foundations of Piety and moral Philosophy were not shaken . . . but strengthen'd by Mathematicks, and Natural Philosophy." Those philosophers "who endeavour to overturn the Precepts of Morality, by Weapons drawn from Matter and Motion, may by their own Weapons be both oppos'd and confuted."

All of Cumberland's energies in his huge book were devoted to proving the absolute validity and authority of one moral rule, from which he believed all virtues could be deduced, namely, the rule of universal benevolence. The common good is the supreme law for all, Cumberland proposed to show, and therefore it is incumbent upon everyone to act to the utmost of their power to promote this good. Only from such conduct can the maximum happiness of each be achieved. The rule of universal benevolence is rationally justifiable, it is the highest virtue and greatest good, it is beautiful, it produces happiness, it is enjoined by God implicitly in the "nature of things," and explicitly in revelation.

Cumberland's proofs for all this were both deductive and empirical. The first, the rationalistic defense of natural law, formulated very much like Rousseau's concept of the general will in the next century, was one of the main influences on Samuel Clarke (1675–1729), the widely-read and -cited Boyle lecturer. The empirical defense, based mainly on an analysis of human nature, fed into the ethics of sentiment that we find later in Shaftesbury. We will look first at the rationalistic proofs, then the empirical argument.

A survey of the conditions on which mankind depends and of the effects of human actions of diverse kinds, remote as well as immediate, leads inevitably to the realization in a rational agent that an individual person is but a tiny part of the human race and that individual well-being is dependent upon the condition of the whole society of rational beings. All men recognize that, in general, selfish behavior cannot lead to the happiness of all, in the same way that they recognize that when several armies are brought into contention, all cannot win. We know that one will win, and the others lose. It then becomes apparent that the common good "is the only End, in the pursuit whereof all Rational Beings can agree among themselves." Such a priori conclusions are forced upon mankind by the "nature of things" themselves.

To perceive in "Men a Likeness of Nature and Condition with respect to Necessaries, and to infer from what is done to others, what we are to hope or fear will be done to ourselves, are Acts Natural and Universal."

Men are influenced by these sensible realizations not less effectively, Cumberland argued, than "mutual Contact between Bodies moving and moved" communicates "Motion among the Parts of a corporeal system." We are immediately obliged by the nature of things to acknowledge "That the mutual good Offices of all are useful to all, Just as natural Bodies in the same System cannot perform their Motions, unless other Bodies concur with, and give place to, them." From the necessity of mutual duties, it follows necessarily, "That he that would, to the utmost of his Power, provide for his own Happiness, must, according to the measure of his Ability, procure to himself the Benevolence and Assistance of all others."

The truths of nature, which reveal God's purposes, are thus imprinted on man's reason. Right reason is itself measured by the nature of things. The structure of nature is sufficient to provide the common and objective standard by which moral good can be tested and tried. Moreover, it follows from the nature of right reason that whoever determines his judgment and will in accordance with it "must agree with all others, who judge according to right Reason in the same Matter." This necessary harmony of right reasons Cumberland called "the fundamental Corner-stone of the Temple of Concord." Like Rousseau's general will, Cumberland's right reason is the moral will of all, the only principle of willing on which all can possibly agree. Cumberland saw this rule as so firmly established that God Himself cannot change it:

> The exercise of Benevolence . . . does as naturally and necessarily produce the private Happiness of every Rational Agent, and the common Happiness of all, as any Natural Cause produces its Effect . . . that is, as two and two make four. . . . A necessity [that is] so Immutable, that neither the Wisdom, nor the Will of God can be thought capable of appointing a contrary Law or Constitution, whilst the Nature of Things remains such as now it is.

The nature of things impresses first principles upon the human mind willy-nilly, from which certain deductions follow in accordance with right reason. In addition to this sort of proof, Cumberland amassed reams of empirical evidence to demonstrate that the model of mutual benevolence is intended by God to be the standard of goodness for men to follow.

These investigations were all put into a teleological context, and it is true that without that underpinning Cumberland is left with only an apodictic system without any convincing factual basis. However, belief in divine design sustained most of the philosophical work in this period, and one can only observe about it that as a basis for interpretation it was extraordinarily fruitful—indeed, still may be—contributing as much to human understanding as the concept of blind natural selection that replaced it.

"The whole of what is to be learned of moral philosophy and of natural laws," Cumberland said, "[can be] ultimately resolved into observations of nature that are known by the experience of all, or into conclusions acknowledged and established by true physiologia [i.e., natural science]." Physiologia includes, Cumberland said, not only the phenomena of natural bodies in motion but also the nature of our minds from observation of their workings and perfections. Human nature itself, he wrote in a key formulation, "suggests certain Rules of Life," and it is possible to find out "for what kind of Action Man is fitted by his inward Frame." It was certain to Cumberland that man was created "for much nobler Purposes, than only to preserve the Life of one inconsiderable Animal." It is in Cumberland that we see first the tremendous influence of the Cartesian concept of system on moral thought in this period. The circulation of the blood is a system, the function of the body's organs is a system, plants and animals are systems, and the whole universe is a system. In all of this, Cumberland believed, the same cooperative relationship of parts to whole applies. The "exquisite machine" of the "system of the world" revealed by Descartes was an inspiration to moralists. In direct opposition to Hobbes, who propounded the egoist or pessimistic concept of human nature, Cumberland reviewed the animal kingdom and much other physical and anatomical evidence and introduced the image of universal benevolence into British ethics. Man is by nature, Cumberland argued, "fitted for greater Benevolence toward those of his own species, than any other kind of Animal is."

To summarize, Cumberland is significant not so much for the development of any one line of thought that was later influential but for the remarkable suggestiveness of the dozens of ideas he spun out that would quickly be woven into the fabric of the new moral philosophy. He was a pioneer in the philosophy of benevolism, a proto-eighteenth-century rationalist, a proto-sentimentalist, and a proto-utilitarian.

Cumberland's French contemporary Nicolas Malebranche was a greater philosopher and is better known, but Malebranche's influence in England (and, I believe, America) is usually underestimated. *The Search After Truth* as a treatise in the new logic was eventually submerged by Locke's *Essay Concerning Human Understanding*, but Malebranche's rationalism and idealism foreshadowed the predominant trend in eighteenth-century American thought, not Locke's sensationalism and empiricism. There is considerable evidence of the esteem in which Malebranche was held for fifty years in British thought, despite his Catholicism, which can only be suggested here. It is widely acknowledged that Malebranche was the greatest of the Cartesians and one of the most original minds of the seventeenth century, especially in his analyses of human faculties and of the passions. The late-eighteenth-century Scottish philosopher Dugald Stewart, reflecting on Malebranche's precipitate decline after being so much admired in Britain, correctly identified him as "the indisputable author of some of the most refined speculations claimed by theorists of the eighteenth century," and believed that Malebranche "contributed a greater number of remarks than Locke himself" to the fund of "practical knowledge of the human understanding." Of course, Locke himself had learned much from Malebranche as well as from Descartes and Arnauld, but he characteristically did not acknowledge his sources.

Malebranche was more theologically involved than Cumberland and was not engaged, as so many English philosophers were in the seventeenth century, in trying to answer Hobbes in the "Malmesbury devil's" own naturalistic terms. Indeed, the union of philosophy and theology was one of Malebranche's ideals, but under the Cartesian influence, his philosophical theology was so untraditional in comparison to the Catholic philosophical theology that preceded him that it was of a different order, altogether, and pointed much more to the future than to the Scholastic past. Like Cumberland he was inspired by Descartes to study nature anew in the simple terms of matter and motion, but also, above all, to use deductive and geometric reasoning, freed of errors, to arrive at truth.

*The Search After Truth* was not written to be a treatise in morals, yet because Malebranche took it as his task to treat "the whole Mind of Man," and believed that "the finest, the most agreeable, and most necessary Knowledge, is undoubtedly the Knowledge of our selves," holding that "of all Humane Sciences, the Science of Man is the most worthy of Man," his book had many valuable contributions to make to moral philosophy, as he himself knew.

Malebranche's most original contribution to the re-conceptualizing of moral philosophy was his theory of the will. Like Descartes, Malebranche purported to dispense with the entire textual tradition that preceded him, finding nearly all prior philosophical speculation riddled with errors, the regular occurrence of false methods leading to false conclusions. A sure foundation for truth could be secured only by proceeding in accordance with Descartes's critical method. One must begin with clear and distinct ideas and accept as truth only what is absolutely evident or can be logically deduced from such evident ideas. The error of trusting the senses, which give only the appearances of things and usually mislead, was constantly emphasized by Malebranche. In effect, proper definitions, as in geometry, are the main source of truth. Malebranche was also half-consciously guided by aesthetic preconceptions about the ordering of the created world. His system has a symmetry about it that he supplied out of both need and conviction.

Mind may be divided into the two traditional faculties of understanding and will. Malebranche saw in these two faculties a nice parallel to the nature of matter, which may similarly be distinguished into the two properties of "receptibility" to different figures and a capacity for motion. By "figure" Malebranche meant simply that matter can be put into different external shapes—a lump of wax can be made round or square—and can also have different internal characteristics. Wax is different from iron, but both are material. In an analogous fashion the understanding is modified by ideas, which do not in fact alter the constitution of mind, and by sensations, which somehow affect mind intrinsically. And just as matter is passive with respect to its receptivity to figure but active when it is in motion, so the mind is passive as a recipient of ideas and sensations but active when it wills or inclines.

Carrying the parallel forward, Malebranche was led to argue that just as God is the universal cause of all motions in the material world, so He is also "the General Cause of all the Natural Inclinations in our Minds." Human beings have implanted in them (by divine design, of course) certain general active tendencies, which can be distinguished from immediate acts of will and from evanescent passions or emotions. And just as the motion of a material object would continue in a straight line if it did not meet with an obstacle, so the inclinations that men receive from God are directed originally to nothing other than good and truth but are caused to swerve from their natural path by extraneous factors, which bias them toward relatively evil ends. Malebranche presumed, with great boldness, that all men still possess the original inclination toward "Good in General" that was given to Adam—indeed, he said, it is an inclination that God "continually Impresses on the Mind." However, the human possession of moral liberty, which is not given to matter, enables men to divert the will from its intended path toward God or toward universal Good. It moves instead toward lesser ends that, in fact, can never satisfy the will for long.

There is clearly an Augustinian background to Malebranche's emphasis on the orientation of the will, but there is no doubt that his conception of the mind as "push'd on towards Good in general" was highly original with him and served as the basis in both Britain and France for many later theories of man's inherently benevolent nature. Malebranche, along with Spinoza, is the founder in psychology of a notion of instincts or drives that go beyond simply biological functions such as hunger or sex.

In addition to the inbuilt inclination to good in general, Malebranche posited two other basic, involuntary inclinations in human nature, both of which are necessarily toward more limited ends, ends that are particular aspects of God as good in general. These are, an inclination to the preservation of our individual being and happiness, and an inclination toward other creatures. Thus, men are incessantly bent by three inclinations: a love to good in general, which underlies all willing; self-love; and love of our neighbor. The basic division of the personality into self-love and social-love is one of the dominant ideas of eighteenth-century moral thought, and although Malebranche is not the sole originator, it was he who first categorized these inclinations psychologically and systematized them. The system into which they were fitted was naturalistic in a sense, but also part of a larger theological scheme.

As I noted earlier, Malebranche believed that "the Inclinations of the Mind are in the Spiritual World, what Motion is in the Material World." God introduced motion into matter so that there would be that "Succession of Forms, and that Variety of Bodies, which compose the Beauty of the Universe." In the same way, inclinations create in the spiritual world an opportunity for God to express His attributes. But God cannot create anything antithetical to Himself, and all that exists does so only because God loves it and wills it. Since God is infinitely perfect and powerful, He loves Himself as the highest possible end, and in order to have His creation in harmony with His own will, He impresses upon it a love like His own. It was to Malebranche inconceivable that God would create anything "without inclining it towards himself, or commanding it to Love him above all things; though he may create it Free, and with a Power to withdraw and to stray from him." Humankind is given indelibly, then, a love to Good in general, or God, and this is the principle, the source, the underlying force of all human capacity to will. Even man's loves for countless lesser or particular goods are but a variation of this ultimate form of willing. Even the greatest sinners tend toward God because they necessarily choose what appears to them to be good—and in fact is good—in a limited way—but they err by a failure of judgment in choosing inferior goods. The will to the good itself, to good in general, continues in any case. The devils themselves, Malebranche wrote, "have an Ardent Desire to be Happy, and to possess the Chief Good: And they desire it without Choice, without Deliberation, without Liberty, and by a Necessity of their Nature."

The notion that all moral choice is made under the aspect of good was an old truth, certainly, but in Scholastic formulations choice was never considered a function of a permanent inclination of the soul. The choice of good was a function of intellect, which then commanded the will, and was a case-by-case matter. Malebranche described a vital propensity, a dynamic psychology, in which will and intellect were conjoined in the single notion of inclination. He was anticipated only by Augustine. The natural inclination to God or good in general is the source of all human restlessness, the "eager Thirst, always agitated with Desires, Anxieties, and full of Inquietudes for the Good that [we do] not possess," the incessant pushing forward to search after objects that have the appearance of Good, and that deceive us into believing that they can supply permanent satisfaction.

The choice of particular or limited goods occurs in accordance with the two chief—yet properly secondary—inclinations already mentioned, self-love and love to others. Malebranche reasoned that:

> God neither Creates nor Preserves any Creatures without giving them a Love like unto his. He Loves himself, he Loves us, he Loves all his Creatures: Therefore, he inclines all Humane Minds to Love Him, to Love themselves, and to Love all Creatures.

Enough has been said about the inclination to good in general, the source of the will's disquiet. I will conclude the discussion of Malebranche, then, with a little further explication of the two other natural inclinations. Self-love is also imprinted continually in the will, for God loves each man as one of his works and man can share in that love for himself. The problem, of course, is that men make the mistake of loving themselves more than God, rather than loving themselves only in relation to God. As a result of sin, self-love has increased inordinately, and the pleasure that men should take in the ultimate good is subordinated to passing pleasures and finite goods. Man in a state of sin is so degraded that he cannot even conceive of loving God for Himself but only insofar as He is good for us. Malebranche's analysis of self-love cannot be recounted here in full, but a few points deserve mention. Although he condemned inordinate self-love, he took a realistic view of its place in the world and saw its usefulness. He did not, however, commit the egoistic fallacy of reducing all activity to a form of self-love. A section of his discussion of pleasure, which he regarded as an expression of self-love, illustrates his realism and perceptiveness.

> There are Philosophers who do what they can to perswade Men, that Pleasure is not a Good, and that Pain is not an Evil: That we may be Happy in the midst of the most violent Pains and Unhappy amidst the greatest Pleasures. . . . They should speak the Truth; Pleasure is always a Good, and Pain ever an Evil: But it is not always advantageous to enjoy Pleasure; for it is sometimes profitable to suffer Pain.

Malebranche gave a number of reasons why it is sometimes profitable to shun pleasure, some very ingenious, but he argued nevertheless that "all Pleasure is a Good, and actually makes those Happy that enjoy it, while they enjoy it, and as long as they enjoy it; and all Grief or Pain is an Evil, and . . . makes the person that suffers it unhappy." The martyr cannot be considered happy in this life, nor those suffering persecution. He therefore believed it dangerous to tell men that sensible pleasures are not good, since it is not true, and "at the time of Temptation they discover it to their misfortune." Men must be told instead that sensible pleasures can only make them happy in some limited measure. However, it is difficult to overcome the temptations many pleasures offer without a countervailing greater pleasure that immediately rivals it, which is where Christian teaching may be helpful. Men must be brought to take pleasure in the highest things, not to despise pleasure itself.

It is perhaps worth mentioning here that Cumberland also did not propose the eradication of self-love as a necessary moral goal, and made the important point that it is possible for men to desire at the same time the gratification of both their own interest and that of others. In other words, benevolence does not have to be entirely disinterested. He also reasoned that the very existence of selfish motives for serving the common good, such as the realization that we may personally benefit from what is done in the common interest, is a further "indication from nature" that man is expected by God to serve the common good.

With regard to the third natural inclination, which was equivalent to Cumberland's benevolence, Malebranche saw this social-love in balance with self-love, each autonomous, the two together strengthening each other by the natural sympathy that men have for each other. Men suffer and rejoice with each other, experience themselves in others and others in themselves. Like Cumberland, Malebranche took the natural evidence of man's inclination to love his neighbor as proof that this is God's expectation of men.

> The strongest Natural Union which God has put between us and his Works, is that which unites us with those Men we live with: God has commanded us to Love them like our selves; and that the Love of Choice, by which we love them, may be Firm and Constant, he upholds and strengthens it continually, by a Natural Love which he imprints in us.

Malebranche called for greater study by philosophers of "the Relations which the Author of Nature has put between our Natural Inclinations, in order to Unite us together," as being more worthy of men's enquiries than the relations that exist between bodies, or the relations between minds and bodies. This encouragement to study the social passions was heeded in the next century particularly by the Scots, who were much impressed by Malebranche's work, which is not to say that Malebranche himself did not speculate very perceptively on these matters.

We may now ask, What are some of the common elements in the work of Cumberland and Malebranche that indicate the direction moral thought would take in eighteenth-century Britain and America? The inspiration of natural philosophy is, of course, evident, but it should be noted that this inspiration antedated Newton by a quarter of a century. The philosophical novelty of what both Newton and Locke had to offer has been much exaggerated. (It is a common fault in the writing of intellectual history to regard the standouts at the present time as the standouts in the past. The world is always thicker with good ideas than we normally notice when looking backward.) It is not just achievements in natural science that we see exciting philosophers; rather, it is the evidence of design in nature, which made nature itself into a specific revelation. That nature is the mirror of God was nothing new. But that from a close investigation of nature one could derive clear moral truths, or at least the confirmation of clear moral truths, was an innovation. Because of the revival of Epicureanism in the work of Pierre Gassendi (see, e.g., Walter Charleton's *Physiologia Epicuro-Gassendo-Charltoniana, or, A fabrick of science natural, upon the hypothesis of atoms founded by Epicurus*, 1654) and Thomas Hobbes, a renewed emphasis on order and design in the universe was very prominent in the seventeenth and eighteenth centuries. After citing a variety of impressive anatomical facts, Malebranche expostulated:

> But if we examine the reasons and end of all these things, we shall find therein so much Order and Wisdom, that but a little serious attention will be requisite to convince those Persons, that are the most Wedded to Epicurus and Lucretius, that there is a Providence which rules the World. When I see a Watch, I have reason to conclude that there is an Intelligence, since it is impossible that Chance should have produced and dispersed all its Wheels into order. How then can it be possible, that Chance, and the meeting together of Atoms, shou'd be able so justly, and proportionably, to dispose all those divers Springs, as appear both in Man, and other Animals?

Men could dispense with the particular authority of Scriptural revelation when the moral order was perceived to be written into nature as well. Once the inner harmonies of nature were understood, and the diverse forces in it justified in relation to the unified beauty and functionalism of the whole, it seemed possible for the first time to search for the beneficent rationale of all natural forces, including those that were formerly considered dangerous. In moral philosophy the sanctifying of the passions, the discovery of their moral value, was directly related to the new comprehension of the forces of nature. Since the time of Aristotle, it had been virtual dogma that reason was integral to morality. In the seventeenth century it began to be argued that morality was not so dependent upon reason as had formerly been thought. One sees this notion suggested already in Malebranche's conception of natural inclinations.

Ironically, at the same time that the Aristotelian emphasis on rational deliberation was suffering reversals, the different kind of Cartesian emphasis on reason as a source of moral truth was winning converts. In both Cumberland and Malebranche, and, of course, throughout the eighteenth century, the Cartesian trust in self-evident principles is apparent. It had the great benefit, as is well known, of stimulating fresh thought, the search for new principles, new foundations. It gave rise quickly to a new form of rationalistic or intellectualist ethics, such as that found in Samuel Clarke and William Wollaston, which concentrated on the possibilities of a formal logic of ethical relations. Rather than speaking in terms of the commanding voice of conscience, Cumberland observed, as Clarke would do later, that the mind discovers in itself a disturbing inconsistency "when it determines to act after one manner in relation to itself, and after another manner in relation to others, that partake of the same nature."

Finally, the strong impetus provided by both Cumberland and Malebranche to the philosophy of benevolism—the belief that man has innate tendencies to love his neighbor, equal to or stronger than his tendencies to love himself—had enormous implications for the future. The presumption of human goodness not only changed society, politics, and education; it also changed theology.

# "The Duties of Man As They May Be Deduced from Nature": James Logan's Unpublished Venture into Moral Philosophy, an Analysis

"'Tis our perfection in our humane state to pursue and keep up to the intention and order of nature: And he forfeits his title to humanity who leaves her prescriptions." Logan, "Duties" (chap. 3, p. 8)

## The Project

In November 1734, James Logan, a distinguished public figure in Philadelphia and in the entire province of Pennsylvania, a prosperous merchant, chief justice of the colony between 1731 and 1735, and a scholar and "philosopher," announced in a letter to Peter Collinson in England his intention to prepare a book-length study of moral philosophy.[1] We do not know precisely what was behind this decision.

---

[1] The standard biography of Logan is Frederick B. Tolles, *James Logan and the Culture of Provincial America* (Boston: Little Brown, 1957). Edwin Wolf 2nd, *The Library of James Logan of Philadelphia 1674–1751* (Philadelphia: Loganian Library, 1974), is a mine of incidental information in addition to being the best source for discovering Logan's reading in all fields. Logan was close to Thomas Story, a Quaker missionary, and shared many of his thoughts with him, as is revealed in Norman Penney, ed., "Correspondence of James Logan and Thomas Story, 1724–1741," *Bulletin of Friends Historical Association* 15, no. 2 (Autumn 1926). Logan's scientific papers are published in Roy N. Lokken, "The Scientific Papers of James Logan," *Amer. Phil. Soc. Transactions*, n.s., LXII (1972), part 6. One of the very few sustained comments on Logan in the past forty years is James L. Barone, "James Logan and Gilbert Tennent: Enlightened Classicist versus Awakened Evangelist," *Early American Literature* 21, 103–17 (Fall 1986), but it is primarily a study of divergent rhetorical techniques. Deserving of attention are two articles by E. Gordon Alderfer: "The Political Career of a Colonial Scholar," *Pennsylvania History* 24, 34–54 (January 1957), and "James Logan: Patron and Natural Philosopher," *Pennsylvania History* 24, 101–20 (April 1957). See also the calendar of a 2014 conference, "James Logan and the Networks of Atlantic Culture and Politics, 1699–1751": https://librarycompany.org/jameslogan/. Logan's competence as a lawyer is illustrated in a short piece by him in Jack P. Greene and Craig B. Yirush, eds., *Exploring the Bounds of Liberty*, vol. 1 (Carmel, IN: Liberty Fund, 2018), 573–93. Most of Logan's letters to Collinson between 1736 and 1741 were transcribed by Edwin Wolf 2nd, who generously granted me permission to use his typescripts. Logan's Letterbooks A, B, and C, from which these transcriptions come, are the property of the Historical Society of Pennsylvania.

Logan's homework in the foundations of law and justice during his stint as a judge was probably one stimulus. Well before 1734, however, he had read William Wollaston's *The Religion of Nature Delineated*, a work with an extraordinary vogue in Britain and America in the first half of the century, and in his November letter to Collinson he indicated that Wollaston was to be a model of sorts: "I have reason to doubt whether I may ever be able to carry [the projected book] to any length worth notice, but from the light this scheme (which I lay deeper than any other I have seen has done) has . . . appeared in to me, I think it were a pity, it should be quite lost, for were it but tolerably delineated, as Wollaston calls it, others more capable might possibly afterwards take it up, and carry it to a just length."[2]

In about 1730, a few years before the letter to Collinson, Logan had also read Francis Hutcheson's *An Inquiry into the Original of Our Ideas of Beauty and Virtue* (London, 1725), a hugely influential work.[3] Thus, whatever may have been his personal motives, the timing of Logan's interest in publishing on the subject of moral philosophy falls neatly into the blossom period of British ethical thought, namely the decade between 1724, when Wollaston's book was first publicly issued, and 1734, when Hume, at age 23, began work in earnest on his *A Treatise on Human Nature*.[4]

Logan's rather diffident ambition of merely "delineating" a scheme of moral philosophy, which he hoped others would develop, as well as his doubts about ever completing it, probably reflected above all his relatively advanced age, for he was sixty in 1734 with some disabilities. His belief that he saw a way to lay the foundations of morality deeper than anyone else before him had been able to do reflected the optimism and naiveté of the amateur and the provincial.

---

[2] Wollaston initially published *The Religion of Nature* privately, in 1722. The first sizable printing was in 1724. Nine editions appeared before 1760. Logan read the book in 1726. He wrote enthusiastically to William Burnet, Governor of New York, on November 7, 1726: "To my very great pleasure, I have lately seen the Religion of Nature Delineated, a piece for which one may justly, I hope, congratulate the age. Both the man, and the work appear equally wonderfull to me, the latter for its own excellency, and the first that a person of such great abilities, such vast strength of thought and erudition, should so long lie obscurely concealed in such a nation" (quoted in Wolf, ed., *Logan's Library*, 525). In a letter to William Reading, July 12, 1727, Logan said that he read Wollaston's book "with an exquisite pleasure" (ibid., 525). On the popularity of Wollaston among the learned in British America, see Norman Fiering, *Jonathan Edwards's Moral Thought and Its British Context* (Chapel Hill, NC: University of North Carolina Press, 1981), 132–35.

[3] Wolf, *Logan's Library*, 242.

[4] It would be hard to find anywhere another ten years so fecund in the study of ethics. Hutcheson's *Inquiry* was published in 1725; Bishop Butler's *Fifteen Sermons* in 1726; the first English translation of Richard Cumberland's great *Treatise of the Laws of Nature* in 1727; John Balguy's attack on Hutcheson in 1728, and Hutcheson's second book, the *Essay on the Nature and Conduct of the Passions and Illustrations Upon the Moral Sense* in the same year; John Gay's short "Dissertation concerning the Fundamental Principle of Virtue or Morality," often pointed to as the first clear statement of utilitarianism (cf. Elie Halévy, *The Growth of Philosophic Radicalism*, trans. Mary Morris [Boston, 1955], 7), appeared in 1731 at the same time as Ralph Cudworth's *Treatise Concerning Eternal and Immutable Morality*, the work of a major figure among the Cambridge Platonists which lay in manuscript for more than forty years; and in 1732 Bishop Berkeley's *Alciphron, or The Minute Philosopher,* written when Berkeley was living in Rhode Island. The translations of the seventeenth-century works were no accident. Cumberland's translator, John Maxwell, prepared a massive edition that with frontmatter, appendices, and annotation beamed the book directly at the discussions in his own time.

Logan lived in an age when aristocrats still felt ambivalent about leaping into print. Unsolicited book publication was acceptable for ambitious comers, such as Benjamin Franklin, but for those already securely located in society and who had money and prestige sufficient, it was more decorous to circulate works in manuscript, or at most to have pieces privately printed. It was not exactly clear in Logan's time, in other words, whether one was elevated by publishing a book of philosophy or demeaned. Because of this ambivalence, Logan went to great lengths to demonstrate his disinterestedness and the purity of his regard for public benefit as his motivation. In a letter to Collinson in July 1736, which clearly evinced some uncertainty about the justification of his undertaking, Logan went so far as to speculate that he might "perhaps be found deficient" in his sense of duty to mankind "if he suffer[ed] his ideas to die with himself." Although such statements are easily dismissed as the conventional masks of ambition, the actual dynamics of Logan's motives and counter-motives are not so readily discovered. Certainly, he was vain about his learning, a fault that was accentuated by the multitudes of uneducated Americans all around him, and he was deeply desirous of proving himself as a scholar and scientist in the international republic of letters.[5] But he also condemned in himself a pride in achievement insofar as this pride conflicted with Quaker standards of humility.[6] Certainly, it must be stressed, Logan was not alone in this particular ambition. The undermining of both religious and Classical authority in the seventeenth century, exemplified by such figures as Descartes, Hobbes, and Spinoza, made urgent the task of reformulating the foundations of morality.[7] In the British American colonies some of the best minds, notably Samuel Johnson of Connecticut (the first president of King's College, later Columbia University) and Jonathan Edwards, published on the subject. Although Logan's work was not circulated in the British colonies, and he cannot easily be fitted into a British American cultural context, it is notable that he was a pioneering secular

---

[5] The variety of Logan's scholarly interests and his competence in many fields comes through impressively in the annotation to Wolf, ed., *Logan's Library*. He published short pieces on botany, classics, mathematics, optics, and so on, in the *Philosophical Transactions of the Royal Society* and other learned journals, but the "Duties of Man" was his most ambitious scheme. In a letter to William Jones, dated March 31, 1738, Logan said that two years earlier he had resolved to give up further study in mathematics. It appears from the timing that he turned from math to ethics, but for him, and others at that moment, those two disciplines were not entirely unrelated. See Roy Lokken, "Scientific Papers," 66. It is hard to find any other person in the British colonies in ca. 1735 who was as widely learned as Logan. He probably had no equal in British North America as a mathematician; he did original research in plant botany, in particular on wind pollination, that was published in learned journals in Europe; he was accomplished in optics and astronomy. He knew the Classical languages and three or four modern European languages.

[6] Logan to Collinson, July 12, 1736, Letterbook A, transcribed by Wolf. On hesitancy to publish, cf. the following comments in Louis B. Wright, "Richard Lee II, a Belated Elizabethan in Virginia," *Huntington Library Quarterly* II (Oct. 1938), 19: "One of the considerations which help to explain the scantiness of literary production in colonial Virginia is undoubtedly an inherited feeling, among the educated aristocracy, that writing for the public press somehow smacked of unbecoming professionalism." Lee and others "probably would have felt it indecorous and unbecoming to run to the printing house" with their "innermost thoughts."

[7] See Norman Fiering, *Moral Philosophy at Seventeenth-Century Harvard: A Discipline in Transition* (Chapel Hill, NC: University of North Carolina Press, 1981).

philosopher on these shores, years ahead of Johnson, born twenty-two years after Logan, and Edwards, born twenty-nine years after Logan. Benjamin Franklin, with whom Logan sometimes conversed, was thirty-two years his junior.[8]

The bare facts are that between 1734 and 1737 Logan wrote a draft of six or seven chapters for a book to be entitled "The Duties of Man As They May Be Deduced from Nature" and ended up by leaving all of it in various stages of revision or incompletion in manuscript. He contented himself with publishing only a short summary of his moral ideas, the *Charge . . . from the Bench to the Grand Inquest . . . held for . . . Philadelphia* (1736; London, 1737), which, like a sermon, was printed as a formality.[9] Logan's concern over the problems of ethics was the generalized concern of the age, as is manifested by hundreds of indications in European culture at the time. What may be called the "problem of virtue" was a major preoccupation of thinking men in the first half of the eighteenth century. It was widely sensed that the clergy's hold over social mores was gradually weakening; that the theological and philosophical syntheses that had sustained moral belief since the Middle Ages were somehow coming apart; that the Scriptures had diminished in authority; and that relativism, cynicism, and other threatening points of view were receiving more of a hearing than had ever been the case before in Christian memory. The outcome was a period of pervasive moral anxiety, the fear that the fabric of traditional moral culture will altogether unravel unless ethical standards are reaffirmed and solidified, and a new consensus achieved. In short, the first half of the eighteenth century was a period of unprecedented creativity in moral philosophy because it seemed to many persons to be a subject of vital and pressing importance.[10]

Logan's effort, then, was indicative of a powerful trend, and it reveals his susceptibility to the intellectual currents of the time. Few good-willed men with intellectual credentials could remain inert in the face of the threats to which Western culture seemed subject from the prevailing confusion in moral standards posed by various forms of deism, Mandevillian cynicism, and the cultural relativism introduced directly or indirectly by both actual and fictional travel literature. The ways and practices, the values and beliefs, of the West, or Christendom, seemed to require justification anew. What prescriptions for social order and the building of individual character were to be followed? To what degree does man live in a universe

---

[8] For the general context of philosophical thinking in early British America, both academic and independent, see Norman Fiering, "Early American Philosophy vs. Philosophy in Early America," *Transactions of the Charles S. Peirce Society*, XIII, no. 3 (Summer, 1977), 216–37.

[9] An earlier publication in the same genre was Logan's *Charge Delivered from the Bench to the Grand-Jury* (1723). The 1736 *Charge* has some significance as a philosophical treatise and is discussed below. Logan sent a copy to Thomas Story and sought his opinion of it, "of the Subject I mean, and not of my performance for that is a matter of indifference to me." For another series of philosophical grand jury charges by a distinguished jurist in America, see L. Lynn Hogue, "An Edition of 'Eight Charges Delivered, At So Many General Sessions, and Gaol Deliveries: Held at Charles Town . . . in the Years 1703, 1704, 1705, 1706, 1707 . . . by Nicholas Trott . . ., Chief Justice of the Province of South Carolina'" (Ph.D. diss., University of Tennessee, 1972). Hogue refers to such "charges" as "a distinct genre with a characteristic combination of hortatory and instructive elements shaped by the immediate goal of justice through the device of a lay jury."

[10] For further elaboration on this point, see the Prologue, above: "The Moral Order from Hobbes to Hutcheson."

sustained by divine moral energy? What is the relation between "nature" and civ-ilized virtue? What are the real consequences of vice? What are the resources in unredeemed human nature for a life of virtue? It was a period when the simple mouthing of the old truths did not suffice to allay anxiety, and when the fate of civilization seemed to hang on the moral education of youth.

The insufficiency of traditional clerical ministrations was revealed above all by the tendency on the part of almost all of the churches to borrow heavily in this period from the formulations of the moral philosophers, even though ironically the philosophers were themselves deeply indebted to the fecundity of seventeenth-century religious thought.[11] But it was moral philosophy drawing on every possible intellectual resource that established the poles of discussion, not theology. It was necessary to probe to the foundations of morality and to define and establish them on solid ground. Neither the ancient classics nor the wealth of Christian literature in the preceding centuries was adequate to the task; thus, the moral philosophy enterprise of the eighteenth century was a unique venture in the history of the West, and, it should be observed, in most respects a successful one. We still live mainly by the postulates in ethics drawn up in the eighteenth century.

If Logan, like others in America and elsewhere, was in fact impelled by considerations such as the above, one may ask: Why then did he ultimately aban-don the effort to address publicly and at length these momentous questions? He gave up his ambitions out of discouragement, it seems, when friends and others to whom he had sent chapters were not wholly uncritical. Since Logan had begun with the idea that he was doing the world a service to write a book on ethics, not surprisingly when the world was at best indifferent to the results he was crushingly disappointed. The problem was compounded by the typical inferiority feelings of the provincial—a note that runs through all of American letters in the colonial period—and even by a fear that a Quaker in particular could never get a respectful hearing. Moreover, as his reading in ethics deepened, inevitably the philosophi-cal complications grew, whereas it had all seemed rather simple at first; he found himself engaged in making arguments against the theories of others rather than writing anything very original on his own part (which he was probably less fitted for in any case). Logan's studiousness and punctiliousness made him a good critic, but he shows little evidence of inventiveness in philosophy.

It is important to recognize, too, how encumbered Logan was with his duties as the representative of the Penn family in the colony and in multiple leadership roles in government, including negotiating endlessly with the surrounding Indians. His biographer, Frederick Tolles, makes that abundantly clear. Logan was also at the same time building a fortune as a fur-trade merchant and engaged in other commercial ventures. These responsibilities were such that one wonders how he found time for his avid and diverse scholarship.

Finally, his advanced age began to tell on him, or so he complained to his friends, and in letters beginning as early as 1736 he intimated that the "Duties of

---

[11] On the subtle translation of the insights of seventeenth-century religious psychology, both Catholic and Protestant, into tenets essential to eighteenth-century secular moral philosophy, see Fiering, *Moral Philosophy at Seventeenth-Century Harvard: A Discipline in Transition* (1981).

Man" might never go beyond the walls of his study.[12] Practically speaking, Logan's difficulties in bringing the work to realization were much intensified by the isolation in which he worked, which was an insurmountable problem. Very few in the colonies were qualified to comment on his work, and to find readers in England and get a reasonably quick reply was a terrible frustration, as will be seen.

All of the pathos of Logan's situation and the practical difficulties he encountered are revealed in his correspondence with Collinson concerning in particular chapter 4 of the "Duties of Man," which was on the passions and affections. The chapter was written probably in the winter of 1735, and late the following spring Logan sent it to England with high hopes. He told Collinson in July 1736 that "having lately looked into some eminent authors on the subject of the affections I begin to have so good an opinion of the sentiments I have there laid down that if their dress will but do I think they may be fit for public view." Logan was particularly proud of his speculations on the physiology of emotion and of his theory that the heart was the organic seat of the passions. (The background for this hypothesis is not relevant here, and we will return to it later.) He suggested, therefore, that Collinson submit the chapter to Richard Mead, an English physician of great renown and a man of impressive learning and wide acquaintance who had on other occasions shown kindness to Americans. A recommendation from Mead, Logan told Collinson, would be convincing "both to a bookseller and to others who perhaps might otherwise be apt to slight any thing from so obscure an author" as himself.[13] Booksellers often doubled as publishers in eighteenth-century London.

A few months later, still enthusiastic, Logan wrote to Collinson, "The more I think of that piece of the affections in which there is so much anatomy which I desired might be viewed and considered by Dr. Mead the more desirous I am it should be done, not that I set any value on it my self but the thoughts being I think wholly new, I could wish the most skilful had an opportunity of considering them." During the same summer Logan did some additional reading on the theory of the passions, "particularly Malbranche's [sic] 5th Book which I had wholly neglected before," and came out with "a better opinion of my own than ever."[14]

---

[12] In a letter to Collinson dated October 3, 1736, Logan already was speaking of his "once intended treatise," even though he continued to revise it for another five years. On July 25, 1737, he wrote to Collinson: "I much question whether ever you will see anything more from me, . . . (for I never expect to finish my once intended Treatise of the Duties of Man as deduced from Nature)." In 1737 he told Thomas Story that he found his "natural abilities much decayed," and on July 5, 1739, Logan referred to his failing memory and observed that he could not "as formerly bear any intense application of thought."

[13] Logan to Collinson, July 12, 1736. On November 15, 1737, Logan wrote to his close friend, the Quaker missionary Thomas Story: "For I have been unfortunate in this, that I have had very few if any acquaintance here, or any correspondents there [i.e., England], who could or would be of use to me" in evaluating philosophical writing. See Norman Penney, ed., "The Correspondence of James Logan and Thomas Story," *Bulletin of Friends Historical Association*, vol. 15, no. 2 (Autumn 1926), 60.

[14] Logan to Collinson, [Aug. or Sept.] 1736. Logan to Josiah Martin, July 12, 1736, in Wolf, ed., *Logan's Library*, 306. On the influence of Malebranche's *Search After Truth,* see the Prologue, above, "The Moral Order from Hobbes to Hutcheson" and Fiering, *Jonathan Edwards's Moral Thought.*

This state of euphoria was not to last, however. Nearly two years passed and Logan had still not heard a word from Dr. Mead. He began to resign himself to the isolation of an American nobody. "I am very little concerned whether he answers me or not," Logan told Collinson in March 1738, putting on a brave face. "The Quaker I have observed on more occasions than one, is a little shocking to them . . . [,] and I am sensible this would be a disadvantage to any thing I should attempt to publish if I should resolve on it."[15] Tell the doctor, Logan then bitterly wrote to Collinson, "that the particular regard I expressed for him in a manner not unworthy the notice of a gentleman and on a subject as little below a physician[,] I thought might have entitled me to the common civility of some kind of answer. . . . If the Dr. cannot believe that either the subject or my self may merit so much of his regard[,] I acquiesce."[16]

Finally, however, after another nine months had elapsed and a total of more than two and a half years of waiting, Logan got a generous reply from Mead, including an apology for the long delay. Logan was pleased that Mead had at last answered, but the substance of the reply was dismaying. Mead rejected Logan's hypothesis that the heart is the seat of the passions and in particular his theory that the unusual number of intercostal nerves leading to the human heart as compared to the nerve structure of animals was proof of this. Moreover, Mead had submitted the theory to colleagues, in particular the celebrated nerve specialist Frank Nicholls, and no one was convinced by Logan's argument.[17]

Logan was compelled to acknowledge to Collinson the collapse of his expectations. "I might perhaps before this time have completed my proposed scheme. But I have reason now to be well satisfied I did not, for my hypothesis, I find, of making the heart the seat of the passions, on which the principal part of that scheme turned, is so generally disapproved by the phisicians . . . that I cannot think it fit the world should be troubled with what is to expect no better a reception." And yet, Logan continued, "I cannot however quite lay down my former opinion."[18]

Despite the anatomical snarl Logan got himself into, there is more to his chapter on the passions and affections than this correspondence indicates. Logan's essay on the passions is the most sophisticated discussion of the subject written in colonial America. Only Jonathan Edwards's book on the religious affections, published in 1746, can be compared to it, but that is a work of a far different nature. In general, it is safe to say that relative to the circumstances of its composition, Logan's entire book manuscript is a remarkable achievement. Had he been living in London or Edinburgh rather than Philadelphia, where he would have had the benefit of immediate criticism of his ideas, and if he had had a bit more leisure, he probably would have developed into a good philosopher, on a level with the large number of British writers who have respectable reputations to this day as contributors to the moral philosophy debate of the era. Logan could not have made a great mark, however, since after Cumberland, Locke, and Hutcheson, who were his principal authorities, he had little that was original to impart. In addition, he did not express himself with superior

---

[15] Logan to Collinson, March 28, 1738.

[16] Logan to Collinson, August 16, 1738.

[17] Logan described Mead's reply in a letter to Peter Collinson, April 5, 1739.

[18] Logan to Collinson, July 25, 1739.

clarity or consistency.[19] Yet by being fated to live and die an American (Logan had come to this country in 1699 when he was in his twenties as an agent of the Penn family), he gained for himself a major place in colonial American culture, viewed retrospectively. Had his "Duties of Man" been brought to print in Philadelphia, Boston, or New York in about 1740, it would have been immediately hailed as an outstanding sign of American cultural growth. Amidst the scanty work in philosophy by early Americans, it is inferior only to Jonathan Edwards's productions. Logan had both a more unconventional and a more vigorous mind than Samuel Johnson of Connecticut, the only other colonial figure with whom he might be compared.[20] Logan lacked Edwards's profundity and logical acumen, and the strength of intellect to remake what he borrowed, but he was a sharp textual critic and particularly impressive for the degree of his conversancy and engagement with British moral philosophy despite all the handicaps of residence in the provinces. "The Duties of Man As They May Be Deduced from Nature" is a work of such magnitude that it changes the configuration of American letters in the first half of the eighteenth century.[21]

---

[19] On the absence of sufficient leisure, Logan wrote to William Jones on July 25, 1737: "My life has been generally a course of business, and the hours I could borrow from that have been employed in a continued variety, I cannot say of study, but of amusement from books promiscuously." Lokken, "Scientific Papers," 66.

[20] As a philosopher in an American context, Logan is on a par roughly with Samuel Johnson of Connecticut, although I believe he had a more critical mind than Johnson. Logan immediately saw the weaknesses in the work of the English theologian John Hutchinson, whereas Johnson was completely taken in. (See Logan's letter to Collinson, Nov. 21, 1738.) As compared to Benjamin Franklin, of course, who was a genius and a brilliant stylist, Logan is pedestrian, but Franklin never tried to write anything systematic beyond a disreputable youthful foray (see the Epilogue, below). Regarding Johnson, see Norman Fiering, "Samuel Johnson and the Circle of Knowledge," *William and Mary Quarterly*, XXVIII (1971), 199–236, and Fiering, "Moral Philosophy in America, 1700–1750, and Its British Context" (Unpubl. Ph.D. diss., Columbia University, 1969), 253–376. Jonathan Edwards had the greatest talent as a philosopher in early America and indeed with few equals in all of American history.

[21] It was not realized until about 1969 that Logan's manuscript survived almost intact in the collections of the Historical Society of Pennsylvania. Frederick Tolles, Logan's biographer, believed that, at best, it was scattered in disarray throughout Logan's papers. Given its documentary value for the understanding of intellectual culture in the colonies, the Historical Society has not lived up to its responsibilities towards Logan's MS in the past fifty years. At one stage in my career, in the 1970s, I aspired to editing the work for publication in book form, but other obligations took precedence and, regrettably, I let that ambition lapse. My complaint is that rather than sponsoring a proper edition by someone qualified, the Society authorized a transcription and publication both online and in print by a person unsuited for the task, Philip Valenti, with the result that knowledge of the work, limited though it is, has been clouded by misinformation and inaccuracies. The transcription itself is marked by serious errors, and yet it is now permanently available, and Valenti's interpretation of the work is, to say the least, chaotic and far off the mark, indeed weird, influenced apparently by the ideology of Lyndon LaRouche. The only rectification of this misstep by the Society, and it would be at best partial, is a new proper printed edition formally endorsed by the Historical Society of Pennsylvania that will repudiate and displace, one hopes, the Valenti edition as a source. The scandal was compounded when Doug Gwyn in *Quaker History*, 102 (Fall 2013), 54–55, as unversed in eighteenth-century intellectual history as Valenti, blithely published a highly favorable review of Valenti's edition of Logan's "Duties." Valenti has published historical pieces in the journal *Executive Intelligence Review*, which is an organ of the political movement led by the late LaRouche. A representative title is: "The Anti-Newtonian Roots of the American Revolution."

Logan's conception of his book was comprehensive and ambitious.[22] The completed work was to have had seven chapters. Chapter 1, which Logan sometimes spoke of as more of an introduction to the whole work than a chapter, was an attack on Hobbes intended to show that "Man was primarily in his nature formed for Society." Logan believed he had discovered several arguments in support of this thesis that were entirely original. However that may be, the general direction of his thinking was in accord with the natural theology of the age that saw in the Creator benevolent intentions, for He had prepared humankind biologically, intrinsically, for a life of virtue, happiness, and cooperation with others. Logan was preceded in this thinking by Henry More, Richard Cumberland, John Ray, and others.

Chapter 2 on the external senses, the organic beginnings of all knowledge, Logan admitted to Collinson contained "nothing quite new."[23] It is, indeed, one of the most unfinished, digressive, and superfluous parts of the book, probably because Logan was too much of an admirer of John Locke to approach the subject freshly. "Solely from the Ideas furnished by [the senses)," he wrote, "We have the first Materials for Thought." This chapter was intended to be a prelude to the next, on the operations of intellect "working" on the data supplied by the senses.[24]

Logan's composition of chapter 3 has a convoluted history, for the author was diverted from his original path by reading, sometime in 1736, Peter Browne's *Procedure, Extent, and Limits of the Human Understanding* (1729), a sharp critique of Locke's epistemology. Browne's book exceedingly disturbed Logan, and the Philadelphia moralist took it upon himself to defend not only his own reasoning but also Locke's honor.[25] Logan particularly resented Browne's fideist severance

---

[22] Logan outlined his plans for the book in two places. Chap. 2, p. 1, of the book manuscript itself contains a description that was written probably in 1735; and also in a letter to Thomas Story, November 15, 1737, Logan reviewed the contents. There are some inconsistencies and confusions, but the outline below is roughly correct.

[23] Logan to Collinson, July [15?], 1737.

[24] Logan first drew a sketch of chapter 2 in the summer of 1734. Five years later, in the summer of 1739, he wrote to Collinson that he had "set about new modeling . . . my 2d Chapter on the Senses." Logan indicated that this second draft was never finished, but beyond the known incompleteness, it seems that some parts of the second draft are also now lost.

[25] In a letter to Collinson on June 8, 1736, Logan blasted Browne, as "(though a Bishop) an insolent abusive and unsupportable Writer full of himself and often egregiously in the wrong and at the same time condemning all our best Writers besides[;] the great Locke's most valuable Essay is in his Language an unwieldy Bulk of Ideal Ignorance and Error[.] Wollaston who had as clear a pen as perhaps ever wrote in English has in his opinion but involved and perplexed the most common and obvious Principles[.] Nor has Dr Clark any better quarter[.] In short his haughty imperious way of treating mankind while he himself is guilty of very gross and palpable errors is so provoking that though I have a very great aversion in my self against charging or attempting to expose any man[,] yet the justice that is due both to truth and merit, oblige me to point out some mistakes in him which all who read what I say must acknowledge [that] these are in themselves of too pernicious a tendency to be suffered to pass un-observed. . . ." "Dr Clark" above is Samuel Clarke (1675–1729), author, among other works, of *A Discourse Concerning the Unalterable Obligations of Natural Religion* (1706). He is described in the Stanford Encyclopedia of Philosophy, an authoritative online publication, as "the most influential British philosopher in the generation between Locke and Berkeley." On his influence in colonial British America, see Fiering, *Jonathan Edwards's Moral Thought*, 87–104.

of morals from all rational proof and his ridiculing of Locke's assertion that ethics could be a science as demonstrable as mathematics. "I observed some errors in [Browne]," Logan wrote to his friend Thomas Story, "of such consequence that I thought it of importance to have them rectified particularly in his Sinking moral Certainty to a degree so far inferior to Mathematical which I think I can clearly shew to be equally built on the same foundation." The attempt to prove the mathematical demonstrability of ethics, one of several quests in this period of moral philosophy comparable to the alchemists' search for the "philosopher's stone," proved beyond Logan's capacities, and the chapter is undeveloped and unsatisfactory. Logan himself explicitly rejected it in the end.

Chapter 4, as we have noted, took up the role of the passions and affections, a subject that had been so intensively canvassed during the preceding one hundred years that Logan was left little room for an original contribution. He contented himself with "some pretty deep Anatomical Speculations in it of the Heart and Nerves" in order to prove that "the Head, which is the only Seat of thought and consequently of Reason, and the Heart the Spring of all Action, are two distinct regions of themselves, tho' of the strictest communication."[26] This tack forced Logan into areas of study, namely anatomy, neurology, and physiology, in which he was not competent, and since the leading physicians of the age were all against him, here, too, he ended up in retreat.

Logan's most remarkable performance from the point of view of American letters may be his chapter 5, written in the spring of 1736, on the foundations in nature for the distinction between moral good and evil. In this chapter he attempted to survey the major schools of thought going back to the natural law theorists of the seventeenth century and culminating in Hutcheson and Wollaston. His purpose was to construct a synthesis, which is not in itself the great merit of the chapter but rather the skill and awareness with which Logan made use of existing literature. The chapter demonstrates, above all, not Logan's strength as an original moral philosopher, which he was not, but his grasp of the subject as it stood in the fourth decade of the eighteenth century. Unfortunately, as was true also of Jonathan Edwards and Samuel Johnson of Connecticut, Logan had not read Bishop Joseph Butler's *Fifteen Sermons* (1726), one of the key works in British ethics of the first half of the century that for some reason was almost unknown in colonial America. Chapter 5 was Logan's last chapter anywhere near completion.

Chapter 6, "Of the Will," exists in a disorganized and fragmentary state of less than a dozen pages, though from this alone the drift of Logan's thought can be roughly determined. And we know that he intended to cap the book with a seventh chapter that would from the preceding conclusions "collectively . . . infer and deduce our respective duties in life, as they will arise to view from these several foundations in nature in our original frame."[27] It is unlikely that he ever wrote any part of this last chapter, but his short, published *Charge to the Grand Inquest of 1736* contains some suggestions that help us to imagine what it would have contained.

---

[26] Norman Penney, ed., "Correspondence of James Logan and Thomas Story, 1724–1741," *Bulletin of Friends Historical Association*, vol. 15, no. 2 (Autumn 1926), 60–62.

[27] Quoted from the outline in "Duties of Man," chap. 2, p. 1.

## The Teleological Method

From the first words of his intended book, it is clear that James Logan was a devotee of the seventeenth- and eighteenth-century pursuit of a system of morals as "natural" as physics. The impetus came primarily from opposition to Hobbes's claim that there is in nature very little, if any, basis for Christian morality, which to some thinkers seemed like an affront to God. What kind of malicious deity would promulgate moral laws in Scripture that the act of creation made almost impossible of attainment! Nature itself, it seemed to many, ought to declare and sustain the divine purposes and standards as much as the revelation of sacred Scripture.

The hunger of this search for a natural morality misled thoughtful men into believing the goal was easily achievable. Logan himself had taken note of the discouraging fact that after two or three millennia of the cultivation of learning, there was still no agreement "on any sure principle on which . . . [to] found the Duties of life and from thence [to] infer and clearly deduce the obligation on mankind to practice them."[28] Why did he then assume that in his day agreement and certainty in morals was more possible than before? Christians had maintained for centuries that the absence of authoritative revelation was exactly the defect that had left pagan thought adrift in a sea of conflicting opinion. What prospects could be hoped for in the eighteenth century without the mooring of the absolute Word? Logan's optimism and the optimism of the era in general sprang from the belief that both a new method and a new source had been discovered. The method was, of course, the Cartesian, which meant generally beginning from scratch with clear, distinct, and self-evident principles and proceeding deductively with extreme care. The new source was "nature" itself, as opposed to inherited textual sources that allegedly had simply multiplied and reinforced the errors of the past. Thus, Logan argued that the cause of previous failure in moral thought was that "inquiries" were not carried "deep enough into nature, in searching and discovering what are the laws originally impressed on man in his formation, which by their inherent force he is impelled to obey; and what are the clear and plain dictates of reason in union with those laws." Logan's program then had two parts: the empirical investigation of human nature to discover the laws intrinsic to man's behavior; and the investigation of mind to discover the primitive elements of rationality that might support a logic of morals. He did not doubt for a minute that these two paths would lead to the same end.

Such a program of investigation was already a half-century old when Logan began to write. The classic formulation in England was that of Richard Cumberland, who in 1672, also in opposition to Hobbes, had laid down as a premise that "The whole of what is to be learned of moral philosophy and of natural laws is ultimately resolvable into observations of nature that are known by the experience of all, or into conclusions acknowledged and established by true natural science." Natural science for Cumberland meant not only the study of the motion and

---

[28] "Duties of Man," chap. 1, p. 1. All subsequent references to the manuscript will appear in parentheses in the text, indicating chapter and page.

behavior of physical bodies, but also the investigation of "the nature of our minds from observation of their workings and proper perfections."[29]

Cumberland was one of the first in modern times to enunciate the general principle that underlies not only Logan's work on ethics but the work of scores of others in the eighteenth century: Human nature, he said, "suggests certain rules of life," and it is possible to find out "for what kind action man is fitted by his inward frame."[30] Like Logan in the next century, Cumberland was looking for both the laws of natural behavior that by their inherent force man is led to obey, and at the same time, for the pure dictates of reason that perfectly complement and describe those natural laws. For the "Author of all" gave man natural moral guidance in two ways: first, by instilling sub-rational inclinations to good ends, and second, by providing him with a capacity for reaching logical conclusions. Nature and reason were coordinate in every detail in this view, a belief we recognize as characteristic of a vein of Enlightenment thought. Rather than conceiving of nature as antithetical to rational order—such as is implied by the Christian doctrine of "fallen" nature—Logan defined it as "the energetic powers implanted in the several parts of the creation by its omnipotent Author, for supporting and continuing them in the order by himself established." "Nature," Logan said, "signifies the same as its divine Author" (chap. 1, p. 2).

Logan considered it part of his task to consider "the whole of man, as a compound of the rational with the irrational," for without this combined study, he said, it cannot be reasonably expected that the natural duties of man can "ever be fully penetrated and justly understood." But his primary concern in chapter 1 was with the non-rational, the affective or instinctive foundations of sociality and benevolence. His starting point, which he assumed would be "universally allowed," is Aristotelian in character and illustrates how easily the "enlightened" mind slipped back into scholastic modes of thought: "It is impossible," he posited, "for any production of nature to be, to act, or to be sensible to, any thing, or to superinduce any new powers, for which nature has not furnished adequate abilities" (chap. 1, p. 1). The point of this obscure statement is simple if the reader accepts its teleological framework. Man's actions or sensations indicate the existence of powers or susceptibilities that exist because they are "natural." These powers, passive or active, are neither more nor less than what is intended by God to be our abilities. Implicit in this idea was something like Leibniz's principle of sufficient reason, though Logan probably knew very little of Leibniz's metaphysics. The existence of anything that might also *not* exist is sufficient reason to assume it was a choice by God. Once this premise was established, Logan was in a position to argue upstream from certain selected human traits to alleged divinely implanted (or natural) intentions in the creation. What *is*, can tell us what *ought* to be.

In conformity with the great natural theology movement of this period, running through John Ray, Robert Boyle, William Derham, Bernard Nieuwentyt, and a number of others all the way to William Paley, who had a major influence on higher education in the colonies, Logan was deeply impressed by the evidence of

---

[29] D. D. Raphael, ed., *British Moralists 1650–1800* (Oxford, 1969), I, para. 106.

[30] *Treatise of the Laws of Nature*, trans. Maxwell, 99.

intelligent and purposeful design in nature. It was an age that despite superficial entertaining of skepticism and positivism had not lost its capacity to wonder at the "intelligence" of nature.

Logan picked a striking example to illustrate his argument, the resemblance and yet the internal differences among the eggs of many creatures. Consider, he said, a large quantity of similar eggs—all smooth, whitish, oval or round, all with apparently simple ingredients, yet out of which comes an astonishing variety of animals: eagles, crocodiles, swans, tortoises, poultry, snakes. All of these animals will be "perfect in their kind," and each will be furnished with "peculiar and distinguishing instincts, by the force of which alone[,] when left to their liberty," they will find their appropriate habitat, mate and reproduce as part of "the grand plot of nature to perpetuate each species," and make proper nests for its young, each following "the exact rules of its species, though having no prior exemplar as to choice of place, materials, methods, etc." (chap. 1, p. 3).

In humans, too, there are inbuilt potentialities, some of which are expressed by the passions. We love and hate, rejoice and grieve, hope or fear, are angry or complacent, because we have "adequate abilities," to use the phrase from Logan's initial premise. Just as we could not walk, work, see, hear, or taste, without feet, hands, eye, ear, palate, etc., so "no more could any of our inward operations be performed, or affections displayed, unless the proper powers for them were truly implanted in us." As with the external sensations, we may regulate and sometimes with application raise these affections by volition, but we "cannot make any one of them for our selves but what virtually and truly, had its roots in us before" (chap. 1, p. 4). As Henry More had commented in the preceding century, the affections "are not from our selves" and cannot be acquired by "thinking or speculation" or by "methods" of any kind. They exist in us "antecedent to all notion and cogitation whatever," and are implanted "as early as life it self."[31]

Logan's initial assumptions, then, were common enough. His next step was to show that man is particularly formed for society and benevolence. Since every quality and disposition found in nature exists for a special purpose, Logan reasoned, each "peculiarly adapted . . . to the ends for which they were severally formed," it follows that all the particulars wherein men differ from lower animals "must in like manner have been intended by the great Author of our being for a peculiar end proper to us alone, who are so distinguished" (chap. 1, p. 5). Every difference in nature, then, can be attached with special teleological significance. Unfortunately, this was a method alive with opportunities for the expression of personal bias, for it put the authority of God at the convenience of any moralist who wanted to make a syllogism. Man can love; therefore, God intended man to love. Yes, but man can also hate.

There was also the problem of distinguishing those traits of man that are cultural products and those that are natural, a difficulty that had magnified enormously in the preceding hundred years as evidence of cultural variety from around the world began to pour into Europe. It was not as easy as it had been to generalize

---

[31] On Henry More's influence in colonial America, see Fiering, *Moral Philosophy at Harvard*, chap. 6.

about "human nature." Locke had taken full advantage of this new evidence in his attack on innate ideas, and both Shaftesbury and Hutcheson struggled to overcome the problem. Logan simply assumed that there was no "sufficient reason" for believing that natural powers varied over time or place in any species, although they might exist in "very different degrees in individuals" and there might be varieties of "modes and pursuits, and of habits contracted from these." But the "root of all is unchangeably still the same without variation," he insisted (chap. 1, p. 4), and he apparently had little doubt that he could find that root.

## The Human Family

What then are the arguments in support of the proposition that man is naturally a social and benevolent animal contra Hobbes? Logan cited about nine, and to his credit not all of them could be found already in Cumberland, Shaftesbury, or Hutcheson, the great sources in his century for "benevolist" argumentation, although a number of these ideas went all the way back to Cicero. Some of Logan's arguments are curiosities indicative of the prejudices of the time and belong in a museum of antiquities. Others could stand reiteration in any age because they reflect perennial humanistic truths.[32]

Logan's first group of propositions pertained especially to the origin of the "kind affections" as they arise and are exercised within "the limits of the family" (chap. 1, p. 11).

1. Only human males, Logan believed, are "touched with the passion we call falling or being in love with one particular alone, and to court one preferably to all others." Thus, humans have a unique drive toward monogamy and prolonged parenthood. As for examples of doves, turtles, and other ostensibly monogamous animals, although they may stay together after mating, "they intirely fail in another great point, viz. in regarding their young after they are . . . enabled," that is, have become self-sufficient (chap. 1, pp. 5–6).

2. There is "a natural coyness" in women, Logan held, "which though some wits are pleased to ridicule and expose under the name of affectation," has in fact a profound purpose. It binds the male to the woman by heightening affection on both sides. Poets have long recognized this instinct, Logan noted, quoting several lines from Book VIII of *Paradise Lost* on the wooing of Eve, and the following from Dryden's libretto for an opera based on *Paradise Lost*, "The State of Innocence": "Somewhat forbids me, which I cannot name/ For ignorant of guilt I fear not shame:/ But some restraining thought, I know not why,/ Tells me you long should beg, I long deny."[33] Since such coyness and resistance is not found in animals, Logan believed, "it is a manifest indication that this special provision in human kind alone was made by nature for strengthening and riveting that

---

[32] I have reorganized, regrouped, and numbered these arguments for convenience and clarity in presentation. None of the substance, of course, has been altered.

[33] *Paradise Lost,* Book VIII, lines 41–48.

tie . . . which is of such vast importance in what is to follow," namely marriage and child-rearing.[34]

3. Marriage itself is biologically reinforced, Logan argued, by the independence of sexual appetite in humans from the female estrus cycle. He reached back to Xenophon's *Memorabilia* in a Latin translation, quoting lines stating in effect that the "Gods take care even for our pleasures; they have determined no season for the loves of men, who may at any time[,] even to their extream old age[,] enjoy a pleasure, which beasts taste not except in a certain season of the year." The point is that the conjugal state is sustained by "a constant Fund for mutual Delight, and the tender Endearments, to soften cares," which continue for life (chap. 1, p. 7).[35]

4. Humans alone have an enduring affection for their offspring, even after repeated parturition. The natural affection in the family is reinforced by the fact that "children, vastly different from the case of all other animals, continue many years unfurnished with either strength or skill to provide for themselves" and remain dependent upon parental care for longer than any other creatures. "'Tis remarkable also," Logan continued, that human breasts in contrast to most other creatures "are placed between the arms; that the mother while her child is sucking may have its face directly in view. . . . By all which means the family is kept more closely together in unity, duty and affection, and the only band of society, mutual benevolence, thereby takes the deepest root" (chap. 1, p. 7). The prolonged helplessness of human beings after birth had been noted for centuries as a unique fact among creatures.[36] Logan's message, of course, was that in the family nest the social affections are cultivated that provide the emotional basis later for the creation of wider social unities. In contrast to this point of view, Jonathan Edwards argued that familial love was inherently selfish and rather than serving as the basis of

---

[34] I have not sought to find out what the majority of anthropologists now say about the meaning and function of courtship patterns in human or animal communities. Logan's point may be restated as follows: the ceremonial accompaniments of human courtship elevate it above mere animal mating and contribute to the seriousness with which marriage is regarded in virtually all human societies. But Logan is surely mistaken in assuming that the courtship is instinctual and thus indirectly strengthens the marriage bond. It would seem more likely that in human society the seriousness with which marriage is taken leads directly and consciously to various elaborations of courtship practices.

[35] *Memorabilia*, I, iv, 12.

[36] A little-known note by A. O. Lovejoy, "The Length of Human Infancy in 18th-Century Thought," *Journal of Philosophy*, XIX (1922), 381–85, calls attention to the use of this argument in Pope's *Essay on Man*, Epistle IV, 11, 125ff; in Bolingbroke's *Fragments or Minutes of Essays;* and in Locke's *Second Treatise on Government,* sections 79–80. The idea is also in Shaftesbury, *Characteristics,* II, 77. Rousseau, in *Discourse on Inequality*, pointed out that the thing to be accounted for is not the steadfastness of the marriage after the child is born, when its evident dependency may indeed strengthen the bond between the parents, but the duration of the union in the months before the child appears. From the point of view of comparative anatomy, the human infant would be expected to spend at least another nine or ten months in the mother's womb before birth. The twentieth-century philosopher Eugen Rosenstock-Huessy has pointed out that human parturition after only nine months in the physical womb ensures that during the balance of time before a stage of physical development is reached equivalent to other mammals at birth, the child lives for another nine months in a spiritual womb, so to speak, namely that provided by the family, which is deeply socializing.

universal benevolence toward mankind, it inhibited it. Yet Edwards was almost unique in denying what was already a truism of the age when Logan was writing: that men naturally move gradually outward in concentric circles to a more and more expansive love of mankind.[37]

5. As a final bit of biological evidence related to family structure, Logan adduced the timing of menopause in women, who become infertile at least twenty years before their natural term of life (unlike females in the animal kingdom, Logan believed). "By this means, they may have full time to raise their youngest and last issue to a proper age to provide for themselves." Logan considered this evidence all the more convincing when it is recalled how this same benevolent design is apparent in the natural affection of grandparents to their grandchildren to a degree "not much inferiour" to their love for their own offspring (chap. 1, p. 8).

The above examples pertained mainly to adult social relations and describe inbuilt supports for sexual harmony and enduring family life. Logan next turned to a body of evidence derivable from individual emotional development that proved in his eyes that man is providentially and naturally a social creature, in particular those "affections and passions" that "manifestly appear to have been implanted in Infants or children, before they are capable of reflection or at least of making any free use of reason" (chap. 1, p. 8).

## Self-love and Society

6. Logan's first example, surprisingly, of a constructive, social affection in children, is self-love. Self-love would seem on the surface to be antithetical to Logan's argument that divine wisdom has implanted in all human beings the necessary and sufficient ingredients for social harmony. Over the centuries thousands of sermons and other Christian commentary had cried up infant selfishness as evidence of inborn sin and pointed to the perpetuation of self-love in adults as a basic cause of human misery. In the course of the seventeenth and eighteenth centuries, however, in one of the most remarkable turnabouts in the history of moral psychology, self-love was gradually neutralized until by the time of Logan's writing, it was already

---

[37] Cf., e.g., Cumberland, *Laws of Nature*, 129. Our sexual drives lead us into monogamy, which in turn lead to offspring and the natural affections of the family. By all this, men and women are inclined to "divest themselves of a contracted Selfishness, which when they have once laid aside, they are easily induced to proceed still further in the love of others, till at last, upon account of their likeness of nature, it takes in all of the same species." This idea, as well as a number of others in Logan's first chapter, may also be found in Pope's *Essay on Man*: "A longer care Man's helpless kind demands;/ That longer care contracts more lasting bands:/ Reflection, Reason, still the ties improve,/ And once extend the int'rest, and the love. . . ." (III, 131–38). Cf. also in Pope, the principle that benevolence moves outward in wider and wider circles (IV, 361–70): "God loves from Whole to Parts: but human soul/ Must rise from Individual to the Whole./ Self-love but serves the virtuous mind to wake,/ As the small pebble stirs the peaceful lake;/ The centre mov'd, a circle strait succeeds,/ Another still, and still another spread,/ Friend, parent, neighbour, first it will embrace,/ His country next, and next all human race,/ Wide and more wide, th' o'erflowings of the mind/ Take ev'ry creature in, of ev'ry kind." Logan described Pope in 1742, as "the brightest genius England ever bred for poetry." See Wolf, ed., *Logan's Library*, 395.

a commonplace to point to its benefits, not only for self-preservation (which God clearly enjoins of man), but also for the preservation of society. The story of this revolution has been expertly told by A. O. Lovejoy. On the purely intellectual level the turnabout was the result of careful analysis and definition, and that rethinking in turn made possible certain transforming distinctions in the meaning of self-love.[38] The exact sources of Logan's treatment of the subject cannot be known, but there is nothing in his discussion that he could not have learned from Pierre Bayle, Locke, and the Third Earl of Shaftesbury, all of whom it is certain he read, not to speak of more detailed treatments of the question that Logan may have known at least indirectly, such as those by a number of French moralists, such as Pierre Nicole or Jacques Abbadie, or English writers like Joseph Butler and Bernard Mandeville.[39] Logan may have been the first American to make the developed case for self-love as a positive benefit, although his comments were brief.

His argument is as follows: Self-love is "highly consistent" with divine wisdom, is necessary in itself, and without it, given the present order of things, a creature would be "exceedingly imperfect and defective." The manifestation of self-love in children takes two forms: a) the desire to get whatever pleases them, which is the same as to say, "whatever in their eyes appears to be good," a trait that Logan does not claim has any direct social benefits, and b) the desire to be praised, or, in other words, the tendency to take pleasure in anything "that shall make them fine in their own eyes and agreeable to those of others." This last trait, widely noted by eighteenth-century moralists, Lovejoy termed "approbativeness," or the human need for approval. Locke's *Thoughts Concerning Education* at the end of the seventeenth century had put particular emphasis on the manipulation of the passions of pride (self-love, self-esteem) and shame as a means of bringing about desirable behavior in children, a method he considered preferable to corporal punishment.[40]

These two forms of self-love, which Logan terms "dispositions or affections," when duly limited by careful upbringing and regulated by reason "must be acknowledged to be of the highest importance in life." The first form of self-love contributes

---

[38] *Reflections on Human Nature* (Baltimore, MD: Johns Hopkins University Press, 1961). Lovejoy was anticipated by F. B. Kaye's introduction to his edition of Mandeville's *Fable of the Bees*, 2 vols. (London, UK: Clarendon/Oxford University Press, 1924). The social and economic causes of the rehabilitation of self-love is a different subject and one that cannot be treated here. For related French thought in the seventeenth century, Paul Bénichou's *Man and Ethics, Studies in French Classicism*, trans. Elizabeth Hughes (New York, 1971; orig. publ. as *Morales du Grand Siècle* [Paris, 1948]) comes closest to showing some of the social foundations of various ethical viewpoints. However much social and economic influences may have shaped the schools of thought, certain of the intellectual outcomes are inexplicable without reference to the inherent dialectic of ideas. For additional discussion of the idea of self-love in the eighteenth century, see Fiering, "The Permutations of Self-Love," in *Jonathan Edwards's Moral Thought*, 150–92.

[39] For French literature in America in this period, see Marie Elena Korey, comp., *The Books of Isaac Norris (1701–1766) at Dickinson College* (1976).

[40] *The Educational Writings of John Locke*, ed. James L. Axtell (Cambridge, 1968), 153. It is probable that Locke borrowed this theme from the French moralists, especially Pierre Nicole, some of whose essays Locke translated into English. Locke emphasized the importance of habit in moral training. Regarding the history of concepts of habit in relation to virtue, see Norman Fiering, "Benjamin Franklin and the Way to Virtue," *American Quarterly*, XXX (July 1978), 199–223.

directly to the immediate sustenance of the child, that is, his self-preservation, "which doubtless was the primary intention [of the Creator] in implanting it." By the second kind of self-love, which may be called self-esteem, children are "naturally incited to improve themselves, acquire worth, and render themselves valuable in the eyes of others." This division corresponds to the distinction current in France in the eighteenth century and made famous by Rousseau, namely that between *amour-de-soi*, or rational self-interest, and *amour propre*, or self-esteem, though the latter idea in particular has many ambiguities. With regard to the second, Locke had written in his *Thoughts on Education*: "Reputation . . . though it be not the true principle and measure of virtue . . . yet it is that, which comes nearest to it: And being the testimony and applause that other people's reason, as it were by a common consent, gives to vertuous and well-ordered actions, it is the proper guide and encouragement of children, till they grow able to judge for themselves, and to find what is right by their own reason."[41] The passion of approbativeness, by making men deeply sensitive to the opinions and standards of their peers, ensures that they will act, paradoxically, in ways beyond their self-interest, and even deny self-interest. Thus, with numerous other moralists in Britain and on the Continent at this time, Logan treated self-love as a marvelous divine dispensation for encouraging virtue, and in this respect he was ahead of his time in the American reception of this idea. Jonathan Edwards, writing in the tradition of Calvinism, was much less positive in his extensive treatment of the subject. Pride, or preoccupation with self, was, after all, in the opinion of many religious thinkers the root sin.

In New England it was not uncommon to accept a limited self-interest as natural to mankind and divinely sanctioned, but it is hard to find anyone before the Founder John Adams who waxed eloquent on the blessings of pride for bringing about both personal achievement and social order. Thus Solomon Stoddard, Jonathan Edwards's father-in-law, in 1717 considered it lawful for men "to aim at themselves in a subordinate way," that is, subordinate to serving God. He also understood as did Edwards later that self-love interpreted simply as the motivational principle of *seeking one's happiness* was inherently ineradicable, which was why Stoddard and Edwards both rejected the Quietest belief that there could be a completely disinterested love of God, or that one could be "willing to be damned for God's sake." Even in the seventeenth century both William Ames and Peter Bulkeley had, like Stoddard later, allowed for limited self-love. "A man in covenant with God," Bulkeley wrote, "may do many things for himself, ayming at the furtherance of his own good both spiritual and temporall, and also ayme at the good of other men . . . in subordination to God and his glory."[42] But in none of these cases was self-love in the form of pride treated as a vital social good.

---

[41] *Educational Writings of John Locke*, 156. Locke's *Some Thoughts Concerning Education* had a far greater readership in early America than any of his other famous works. Historians who speak loosely of Locke's "influence" in America, based on some general reference to "Locke" by a writer, generally fail to specify which of Locke's important books they are talking about, which has caused untold confusion, especially with regard to his specific influence on the Founders.

[42] Quoted in Michael McGiffert, "The Problem of the Covenant in Puritan Thought: Peter Bulkeley's Gospel-Covenant," *New England Historical and Genealogical Register*, CXXX (April 1976), 107–29.

Similarly, during the Great Awakening in the middle colonies a defender of so-called old-side Presbyterianism, John Thomson, lectured the evangelical Gilbert Tennent in 1741 on the fallacies of Tennent's animadversions against self-love: "Self-love," Thomson said, "is so incorporated with our rational constitution, that it's simply impossible for us to renounce it, it is supposed in all the promises and threatenings of the Word, of both Law and Gospel, it is supposed in our happiness, which is joined together with the glory of God, as Mans chief end, in our catechism; and therefore it must be acknowledged to be, tho' not the sole and adequate, yet the partial and adequate foundation, i. e. motive of our obedience."[43]

To some extent, however, Thomson and Tennent were arguing at cross-purposes, since Tennent himself espoused the traditional teaching regarding the legitimacy of limited self-love in his famous sermon on "The Danger of an Unconverted Ministry" (1740) and in several other places: "Natural reason will inform us that good is desireable for its own sake. . . . Evil as evil, or a lesser good, which is comparatively evil, cannot be the object of desire. There is a natural instinct put even into irrational creatures, by the Author of our being, to seek after the greater natural good, as far as they know it. Hence the birds of the air fly to the warmer climates, in order to shun the winter-cold, and also doubtless to get better food."[44] What Tennent meant to emphasize in this confused debate, in contrast to Thomson, was that spiritual regeneration cancels *exclusive* self-interest, or subordinates it to that *inclusive* self-regard that aims at one's own happiness only as part of the glory of God. After conversion, one finds one's happiness in serving and loving God. Neither man expressed the belief that through the transmutation of self-love into concern for personal reputation any good could come. This would be comparable to "loving" God out of a fear of hell. Thomson, however, might have accepted the desire for heaven as a legitimate motive for faith and obedience, whereas Tennent, had he clearly articulated the principle, would undoubtedly have argued that the desire for heaven ought to be the by-product of love for God rather than the cause of it.

A little later in the eighteenth century, Calvinist ministers were still struggling with the problem of self-love. In 1759 Samuel Cooper in Boston attempted a synthesis, but he also did not include approbativeness as an acceptable motive for virtue. "We see that the glory of God and our own happiness ought never to be set in opposition to one another," Cooper preached. "We can never be called to renounce the one for the sake of the other; . . . they are both so strongly enjoyed that if we attain one we infallibly secure the other." This assertion would have been more precise if Cooper had used the phrase "true happiness" rather than just "happiness," for it was the correspondence of *true* happiness with serving the glory of God that he had in mind. "We see," Cooper continued, "that it is not inconsistent with the truest Virtue,

---

[43] Alan Heimert and Perry Miller, eds., *The Great Awakening* (Indianapolis, 1967), 116 . Thomson may have been borrowing from one of the outstanding defenses of self-love in British moral thought, John Clarke's *The Foundation of Morality in Theory and Practice* (York, Eng., 1726), published the same year as Butler's *Fifteen Sermons*.

[44] Heimert and Miller, eds., *Great Awakening*, 87–92. Cf. Gilbert Tennent's "Unsearchable Riches of Christ," preached in 1737: "The desire of happiness is co-natural to the human soul," in ibid., 14–19.

the purest religion to act from a regard to our own welfare; that this motive is natural as well as Christian; and that we ought not to disturb ourselves and suspect our own sincerity purely because we cannot wholly divest ourselves of a principle of self-love."[45] Here, too, the failure to make adequate distinctions—such as those that had been so brilliantly employed by Joseph Butler a quarter of a century earlier—could only have confused Cooper's auditors. In a slightly earlier sermon, Cooper made use of an argument that went back to St. Augustine, namely that Jesus himself "has taught us to make the love of ourselves the measure and standard of love to others."[46] And in accordance with the predominant theory in British moral thought at mid-century, Cooper maintained that if it were possible for "a rational creature, to extinguish the principle of self-love," the result would not be "Vertue or perfection" but rather "a gross and monstrous defect in his constitution." It was the balance of self-love and social virtue that mattered in Cooper's analysis, as in Shaftesbury's. Self-love was as necessary as public virtue and complemented it. But Cooper did not maintain that self-love can and ought to be turned into a social virtue.[47] The metaphor of the balance of the affections, which is very prominent in Hutcheson, is quite different from the claim that self-love is identical to social virtue.

The dangers inherent in Logan's acceptance of the principle of approbativeness as a legitimate expression of self-love were patent. Once trust or advocate this process by which true virtue is so closely imitated, then all sorts of hypocrisy can creep in. The vaunting of self-love, in the sense of approbativeness, as one of the divinely introduced agencies by which God brings good out of evil, appeared to be the tactics of cynicism. In order to sanction this human passion for reputation one had first to despair of the efficacy of spiritual forces to create goodness in man and to give up all hope of a civil state that was undergirded with religion rather than political expediency.

Moreover, historically, it was difficult for any descendant of the Puritans to embrace the ethics of pride. As a Quaker, Logan was in a similar tradition, which makes his espousal of this doctrine all the more surprising. That Locke also accepted it is equally surprising. Paul Bénichou has argued convincingly that the ethics of the Jansenists—which in most details was identical to that of the Puritans—was an outgrowth of a direct refutation of the aristocratic *éthique de la gloire* that was pervasive in France in the seventeenth century. This ethic had made frank use of reputation as a motive for such virtues as courage, magnanimity, honesty, and so on. It may have been effective, but to the Jansenist and the Puritan, the constant reference to *self* was anathema, especially since pride in one's humility was not typical of the nobility. It was the love of personal greatness that moved them.

---

[45] Quoted in Charles Akers, "The Divine Politician: Samuel Cooper of Boston," unpublished manuscript, p. 202.

[46] Jonathan Edwards also believed that Matthew 19:19 indicates that we may and must love ourselves. See Fiering, *Jonathan Edwards's Moral Thought*, chap. 4, "The Permutations of Self-Love."

[47] Quoted by Jack Crowley, *This Sheba, Self: The Conceptualization of Economic Life in Eighteenth-Century America* (Baltimore, MD: Johns Hopkins University, 1974), 91, from Cooper's *Sermon Preached in Boston . . . before the Society for Encouraging Industry and Employing the Poor* (Boston, 1753), 2.

The Jansenists, like the Puritans, reveled in showing the inner corruption that the *éthique de la gloire* promoted and in contrasting it with Christian sanctity. The motive of glory itself was shown to be mere base pride. But, ironically, the very explorations in the subtle convolutions of self-love in which the religious opposition had pioneered for the sake of exposing to censure the ethics of the aristocracy became the basis later of the directly opposite positive teaching. The general outcome was the argument that politics and society require both the passion of approbativeness and the passions of pride and self-esteem. Both are good and necessary, otherwise God would not have put them there.

Shaftesbury and Hutcheson were aware, of course, of the efficacy of pride in simulating virtue. What they denounced was the cynical claim that there was no other virtue possible than this kind, and they worked to establish in moral philosophy the belief in forms of irreducible virtue, that is, virtue that could not be shown to be simply a manifestation of self-love. In this respect the interests of the benevolists corresponded to those of the Calvinist clergy in America, who could not but regard the legitimation of approbativeness or pride as the devil's work, for it threatened to drive out belief in and hope for true and authentic Christian virtue and in the end equate true charity with hypocrisy. James Logan, in fact, did not advance the notion that there was no other virtue beyond that which can be reduced to self-love. On the contrary, he argued strenuously in chapters 4 and 5 of his manuscript for Hutchesonian disinterested benevolence. Yet his attribution of providential origins to the passion for praise and social distinction was in contradiction to that intent.

In the conclusion of his short note on self-love, Logan issued the usual cautions. These excellent dispositions, he said, which are necessary for human well-being, are subject to terrible corruption when not duly governed "by the powers of reason." When carried to excess, they are capable of degeneration into avarice, base pride, and ambition, the "grand sources of most of the miseries and calamities of human kind" (chap. 1, p. 9).

## The Social Affections

7. Self-love and its benign consequences are not the only natural dispositions found in children that direct them ultimately to social harmony. The passions of anger, love, and gratitude also contribute. Anger is implanted in all animal-kind, Logan believed, as necessary "to prevent injuries" and to protect the "safety and well-being of the individual." Logan was simply arguing here in accordance with the trend toward a teleological interpretation of the passions instigated by Descartes and carried forward by Malebranche, Henry More, and others. Apparently, Logan saw anger as a principle of order in society, a passion in men that suits them for social life by setting limits on the intrusions of others. Like self-love in its primary form, however, anger does not benefit society in general. But by contributing to individual well-being, it adds to the total of social good. In Logan's use of it, it is closely related to self-preservation.[48]

---

[48] For more on the question of the moral value of anger, see Fiering, *Jonathan Edwards's Moral Thought*, pp. 187–189.

Love, on the contrary, offers direct social benefits, and Logan believed that it was "designed to have the most exalted empire" in the human breast, and "were it duly nurtured, and not checked by other prevailing passions, it would exert its self to a degree that would sweeten every other affection, render life truly a blessing and raise mankind to the perfection first intended for him in his formation." Love appears early and strong in children, Logan observed, and is given by them readily not only to parents but to other benefactors. Closely related to love and equally natural is the "principle of gratitude."

Finally, Logan mentioned compassion, in which, he said, young children are not deficient. They show a natural interest in their peers, and when one is punished or they see another grieve for any reason, "compassion will immediately arise, and shew itself in tears and cries" (chap. 1, p. 9). All of these examples had already been cited by Francis Hutcheson.[49]

Logan did not assume, of course, that all children exhibit these constructive and desirable traits in the right measure. As with trees and animals, some are found "much more defective in particular abilities, qualities or dispositions, than others." Some children appear to be "insensible to all the tender emotions and sentiments of love and compassion." And what begins as "an unhappy defect in their nature" is reinforced by acquired habits until the vices opposite to the charitable qualities are "exceedingly strengthened." When such native dispositions and habits are found in conjunction with strong abilities of intellect or other outward advantages, such people become "the plagues and enemies of mankind" (chap. 1, p. 10).

But despite these exceptions, Logan adhered to the view that the cited evidence "irrefragably proves" that "Nature has peculiarly provided these determinate laws for men: That families should commence and be continued by the strongest ties of affection in conjugal, parental, filial and fraternal love: And that on the first discovery of our passions, together with that love which every individual must necessarily bear to it self for its own preservation; this affection also discovers it self . . . more generally to other like objects and to benefactors." The social affections of love, gratitude, and compassion, Logan said, are "truly founded in our natures, and as clearly manifested to be inherent in our compositions as any instinct can be discovered in any animals whatsoever" (chap. 1, p. 10).

The difference between men and animals, however, is that men are not governed unfailingly by instincts (chap. 1, p. 11). They act sometimes from principles other than the kind affections and have been guilty even of the "greatest barbarities" to their nearest relations. The explanation for these aberrations lies in the "perverse use" men make of that free will, given to them as a necessary accompaniment to the noble power of reason, "from which alone our species derives all its excellency and superiority." Logan was convinced that without freedom, human beings "could not be accountable, could have no merit, nor become the proper objects of either rewards or punishments." But free will also allows for the abuse of reason, a problem that creatures guided by instincts do not have. Human affections

---

[49] See, e.g., L. A. Selby-Bigge, ed., *British Moralists*, paras. 145–149, 156–157. See also, Norman Fiering, "Irresistible Compassion: An Aspect of Eighteenth-century Sympathy and Humanitarianism," *Journal of the History of Ideas*, XXXVII (April–June, 1976), pp. 195–218.

can do no more than "silently" point out or at least "incline" us to our duty, and "render the discharge of it easie and truly delightful" (chap. 1, p. 11).

Logan's analysis of the will did not come until his chapter 6, which was never completed, and he nowhere discussed the problem of such freedom in any depth. Thus, this remains one of his very few statements on the subject. It is clear from these passages, however, that he was attempting somehow to unite an intellectualist theory of moral government and duty with Hutchesonian sentimentalism. The effect is to leave the reader in doubt about the relationship of reason and duty to the kind affections. Hutcheson had maintained that vice or wickedness was the result not so much of a defect in rational control as of the strength of contrary passions. With this theory, which was more consistent with Logan's earlier essentially determinist arguments, the American never came to grips.

The last two items in Logan's catalog of the evidences for man's natural sociality dealt with the incest taboo and the faculty of speech. Although here, too, there was nothing entirely original, the variety of Logan's arguments and the absence of the most predictable conformity to the usual paths in his handling of the issues, seems particularly impressive in an American writer at this date. This characteristic may be accounted for, perhaps, by the vast learning that Logan had stored away, or, in other words, the range of his textual scholarship, which was certainly unusual in British America, and unmatched, it would seem, by any figure in the colonial period other than Cotton Mather in an earlier generation.

## *The Incest Taboo*

8. Logan was deeply interested in the means by which love between brothers and sisters is superseded by later heterosexual relations between non-kin. The teleological approach might lead to the assumption that the strong affections often seen between brothers and sisters indicates that nature intends for them to cohabit for life. Yet nature has taken care to order it vastly otherwise, Logan claimed. For opposed to that natural affection between siblings, nature "has implanted an abhorrence and utter reluctancy to the thought of entering into the conjugal union under that relation" (chap. 1, p. 12). We find instead that the early affections already described "run not only out of the family, but frequently to strangers, and sometimes to persons never known or seen before[,] towards whom a stronger affection commonly arises and more imperious, than all the others together." Logan considered the law against incest a universal trait that even the most barbarous of men observe, as opposed to mere animals. And this repugnance to incest creates in turn the conditions under which kind affections among siblings is transferred to the love of outsiders and becomes the basis of marriage.[50]

---

[50] Cumberland, *Laws of Nature*, 337ff., had presented the same argument: "The business and tendency of the known laws of chastity, both in a single and married state, is, not only to benefit the minds and bodies of the chaste; but to found new families, to preserve old ones, and to extend friendships, rising from affinity by marriage; whence arises a closer union and society between the parts of the same State, and also between members of different States, and, consequently, of all mankind." Cumberland then cited the incest prohibition as a specific example. "Natural reason," he said, has "instructed almost all nations" of this rule.

On this subject in particular Logan had to contend with the challenge of both historical and cultural relativism. At different times in history, in various places, and under particular circumstances incest does seem to have been permitted although still a taboo. Logan was aware of the common historical examples. In his original draft of chapter 1 he mentioned instances from Persia and Egypt, and cited Catullus's poems attacking Gellius. Then in an addendum to the chapter, written probably in the summer of 1740,[51] he listed many more instances from antiquity. The addendum was designed specifically to counter objections to Logan's argument that there is a "natural aversion to a conjugal union between brothers and sisters" and that this aversion is divinely ordained in order to encourage the extension of love beyond the family setting.

The main thrust of Logan's reply to those who were skeptical of his thesis was essentially a primitivist argument. All manner of trespasses and violations of nature occur, but "no where more than in those nations called civilized," where "pomp and magnificence, luxury and cloathing," and so forth, creates an environment in which "simple nature" is "scorned as too mean to give laws to its own productions." In the same countries where incest was found there were usually other unnatural practices, such as castration, "mewing up [i.e., confining] of women," murdering of brothers, and the like (chap. 1, p. 12).

The real question is, Logan said (following Shaftesbury and Hutcheson to the letter), regardless of the practices in certain exceptionable places and times, "What are the pure and genuine dictates of nature, from her implanted laws, when not contravened or corrupted?" Shaftesbury had spoken of unnatural affections that could not be used as a standard of behavior, for they represented mere perversions of the grand design. Hutcheson had pointed out that "Though men hold and act on stupid and ridiculous opinions all over the world, no one denies the universality of reason in men."[52] Why then make exceptions the basis of a denial of other natural traits? It is clear, according to Logan, that the great "design" of the natural resistance to incest is that "those kind affections which are the true and natural foundation of society should not be confined to the limits of one family, or within the narrow compass of those ties of consanguinity, but should be directed to strangers or new objects [in order] that more families should be united in affection" (chap. 1, p. 13). The proscription of incest, then, became for Logan one more instance of the means by which natural affections ensured that "Benevolence should be universally diffused, and take in our whole species though not all in equal degrees" (chap. 1, p. 13).

## Other Natural Evidence

9. Finally, aside from the witness of the affections, there is still other evidence derivable from the study of the unique characteristics of human nature that can serve as a guide for standards of morality. "Mankind is the only species to whom the gift of speech has been indulged." Logan credited Locke with the suggestion

---

[51] Logan to Peter Collinson, Aug. 1, 1741.

[52] Hutcheson, *Inquiry*, 183.

that "the perfect distinction between mankind and brutes consists in this, that the latter are not capable of forming abstracted or universal ideas" (chap. 1, pp. 14–15). But it is not necessary to go so far as this, Logan proposed. We may, he said, fix the difference "in their not being capable of reflecting at all on their ideas received from sensible and outward objects." Today we might speak of man's unique capacity to use symbolic forms. The point about speech is that its sole use is in company and conversation, according to Logan. Society could not exist without it. "The grant itself therefore, of this faculty to humane kind alone, evidently shews it was designed by nature that men by means of this should commune together, impart their thoughts, and express their sentiments arising from the affections implanted by nature, as well as reason together and agree on measures for carrying on, by mutual aid, the necessary affairs of life."

In addition to the power of speech, man has other means of communing. No other species "have any such muscles in their faces as are capable of giving any remarkably distinguishing alterations to their countenances. But in man a provision has been made of these so very largely, that there is scarce one passion can arise in the mind, especially if it be at all sudden, but it may be read as clearly in the countenance, as if it were vocally expressed" (chap. 1, p. 16). A similar observation had been made by Cicero. Logan also mentioned smiles and laughter. These examples and others were commonplaces of humanistic literature, and it is clear that Logan's strengths as a moralist depended in part upon his wide reading in Classical and Renaissance sources.[53]

I have passed over silently a handful of minor arguments adduced by Logan, but the essence of what he had to say appears in the preceding nine sections. If there could be any doubt that he interpreted the world in terms of final causes, it is removed at the end of this first chapter. Everywhere in creation, he summarized, there appears to be "a most exact provision suitably made for man to exercise his industry and abilities upon. . . . For to what other end were those thick fleeces given to the helpless sheep, and some other animals that yearly cast them, when thicker pelts without these loads, such as those of horses, kines, hounds and such like might in all appearance have done as well? For what end was the despicable silk worm formed. . . . For what end are all those exceeding tough rinds of plants the

---

[53] A typical example is Charron's list in *Of Wisdom*, trans. George Stanhope, 3rd ed. (London, 1729), I, 33-31, 41–42: "The body of man hath several very particular and distinguishing qualities, which are excellencies peculiar to himself, and such as beasts have no share at all in." Charron then listed, among others: speech; the hand, "which is a prodigy in nature, and no other creature, not even the ape it self hath any thing comparable to it"; "the sense of being tickled"; laughing and crying; blushing for shame; "multiplying at all times indifferently"; the multitude and unspeakable variety of his dreams, so extreamly above all other animals, that man alone deserves the name of a dreaming creature"; and so on. Charron discoursed at length on the face. "The face is the throne of beauty and of love; seat of smiles, and of kisses, two things peculiar to mankind. . . . [It] is adapted to all manner of changes in the temper; it expresses all the inward motions and passions of the soul. Joy and grief, love or hatred, envy and malice, shame and anger, indignation and jealousy, and the rest of them, immediately betray themselves here. This is like the hand to the watch, which tells us the hours and the minutes, while all the wheels and springs, by which these movements are made, lie within and out of sight. And as the air receives all colours, and all alterations of the weather, and so lets know what changes are coming: So may it be said of the countenance too."

earth produces, as flax and hemp. . . . For what use did the earth furnish minerals?" Logan added many other examples of this sort, including the observation that the ability of wood to float on water rendered deep oceans passable that otherwise might have excluded one part of mankind from any possibility of communicating with the other (chap. 1, p. 18). That a person with a scientific mind of the caliber of Logan's, who comprehended Newton's *Principia* as only few others in America at the time were capable of, and who did significant research in botany, could also adhere to this kind of reasoning, which so easily ends up in absurdities, may seem hard to fathom. But such mixtures of teleology and empiricism were fairly typical in this age. One is never quite sure when Benjamin Franklin is being facetious, but in an essay delivered in 1732 to the Junto, "On the Providence of God in the Government of the World," Franklin argued that the goodness of God appears in his "giving life to so many creatures. . . ; in his providing plentiful sustenance for them all, and making those things that are most useful, most common and easy to be had; such as water necessary for almost every creature's drink; air without which few could subsist; the inexpressible benefits of light and sunshine to almost all animals in general; and to men the most useful vegetables, such as corn, the most useful metals as iron, and the most useful animals, as horses, oxen and sheep, he has made easiest to raise, or procure in quantity or numbers."[54]

Thinkers in the eighteenth century did not find it difficult to take an empirical view of the operations of nature and at the same time retain a naïve metaphysics. It was no small step in thought to look at the earth and all the things in it as having no particular predestined relationship to man, or to look upon the universe as essentially inexplicable, if not purposeless. Moreover, there is no logical inconsistency between interpreting events in terms of both final and efficient causes. The former, however, was becoming more and more superfluous. Nor is there anything wrong with a teleological metaphysics per se. It is when it is introduced to explain minute details about the world that it becomes ridiculous, since so many "meanings" for things are assignable.

Logan's peroration to chapter one expressed the faith of many in his time. Nature itself proclaims to men, he said:

> Behold the vast provision here made for your industry[.] Join together in that love and benevolence that I have implanted in you and by your mutual aid, and united endeavors, render them truly useful. But enjoy them under a due sense of gratitude to your bountiful donor, your Creator and supream Lord of this universe[,] the beautiful and exact order of which, in all its outward parts you here behold. . . . This order you are to imitate in what is left in your own power [,] your wills and your affections[.] This therefore do and be completely happy. (chap. 1, p. 20)

---

[54] *The Papers of Benjamin Franklin*, ed. Leonard Labaree and Whitfield J. Bell, Jr., (New Haven, 1959), I, 265–66. Franklin may have been in a mood to speak conventional pieties in this statement. More facetiously, he also said, or quoted from somewhere, that God in the Creation added a bridge to human noses in order to hold up spectacles. In Pope's *Essay on Man* (1733), such reasoning was already an object of ridicule: "Know, Nature's children all divide her Care;/ The fur that warms a monarch, warm'd a bear./ While man exclaims, 'See all things for my use!'/ 'See man for mine!/ replies a pamper'd goose;/ And just as short of Reason he must fall,/ Who thinks all made for one, not one for all" (chap. 3, pp. 44–48). The Junto was a Philadelphia club that Franklin founded, meeting regularly to discuss matters of practical and intellectual interest.

The first chapter of Logan's "Duties of Man Deduced from Nature" perfectly represented the author's general point of view, both in terms of method and substance. With regard to the latter, Logan indicated his determination to refute the Hobbesian interpretation of man and took his stand with the optimists in psychology. As for his method, it was obedient to the leading principle of the age in the study of moral philosophy: a sound and careful description of human nature is, at the same time, both empirical and a revelation of God's prescriptions for man. Logan intended the first chapter to be an introduction to the work as a whole, for it did not engage in a detailed way with the specific issues in ethics that remained even after the Hobbesian bugbear was done away with. The balance of Logan's manuscript is devoted not so much to the pessimist/optimist (or the egoist/benevolist) controversy as to the intestine quarrels among those who were roughly in agreement on an optimistic view of human nature.

Logan's chapter 2, on the "Exterior Senses," and his chapter 3, on "the Intellect," are the most directly imitative in his book. Their starting point is identical with that of Locke's *Essay Concerning Human Understanding*, namely, that one cannot even begin to do moral philosophy until one's logic (or epistemology, to use the more modern term) is clarified. Before speaking on the right and the good we must know how far human knowledge can extend, and, perhaps, must contend with the question of how we can know anything at all. The investigation of man's intellectual faculties, "so far as they can be discovered to have been in the intention of nature, or more properly speaking of our Creator in framing [them]," and the inquiry into the "purposes" for which they were given to man, and "to what length they can reach, and generally how they are to be applied," is the precondition for attaining "that measure of happiness in social life, which appears to have been intended for us."[55] Logan's goal, exactly like Locke's, was to arrive at a "more just conception of the powers of our intellectual faculties . . . ; for hereby we shall not only be taught in a good measure to see the extent and limits of these faculties, but also discover our ignorance[,] which is scarce of less moment to the just discharge of our duties" (chap. 2, p. 2).

## The Intellectual Faculty

Most of Logan's chapter 2 on the senses we can pass over quickly, for its composition was beset by problems not unlike those he created for himself in chapter 4. Despite his express intention of discussing the senses only as aspects of mind, his inclination toward natural philosophy got the better of him, and he found himself entangled with Newton's theory of light, which he apparently had hopes of slightly improving upon. This investigation bore no fruit, and Logan ended up rejecting that section of the chapter. He also digressed into an admiring description of the anatomy and function of the eye—a favorite subject of natural theologians in the eighteenth century—which Locke, who had a better grasp of his purposes, had refrained from, and even into such matters as the meteorological foundations of the sailors' adage, "Red sky at night. . . ." (chap. 2, pp. 6–10).

---

[55] "Duties of Man," chap. 2, p. 1.

At one point later in his manuscript Logan indicated that he had hoped to demonstrate in chapter 2 that "the internal sensations excited through [the external sense organs] entirely depend on the formation and texture of the organ," which would have been a prodigious, indeed an impossible, achievement given the state of knowledge in the eighteenth century. Moreover, this goal was inconsistent with Logan's original plan of discoursing simply on mental operations in themselves. It is clear that Logan's metaphysical presuppositions were not altogether sorted out before he began the "Duties of Man," for in addition to the providential teleology that we have already encountered, he also claimed in chapter 2 that "all the changes, all the effects produced in the universe are intirely owing to motion; of which there are very many sorts" (chap. 2, p. 11). Although there is no elaboration, the statement suggests a radically mechanistic view of the universe. One thing is definite: Logan completely rejected metaphysical idealism. He accepted the Cartesian reasoning that only a malicious God would give man the impression that external matter is real and yet have it be idea only.[56]

The digressiveness of Logan's chapter 2 appears much more obvious in the twenty-first century than it did in the eighteenth, when natural and moral philosophy constantly interwove, but it is unmistakable, nonetheless, that Logan could not make up his mind about how to proceed. His instinct to dig deeper than was usual, to go beyond even Locke and Newton, was a good one, although one cannot help but feel that the urge in his case was quixotic. Logan dreamed of making a big conquest, it seems, as Franklin succeeded in doing about twelve years later in his experiments with electricity, achieving international renown, but this ambition was fatal to the more realistic possibility of his making instead a small and complete contribution.

In a curious way, however, Logan's aborted chapter 2 bolstered one of his Lockean aims in writing it. The nature of light is so much of a puzzle, he concluded, that Newton himself could not form "any adequate notion of it," and "I was sensible myself of a ne plus ultra in the opposition of unsurmountable adamantic bars." In other words, Logan's exploration of the problems associated with comprehending the nature of light and vision verified for him, as he said in a letter to Collinson, that the "Creation was for the use of, and to be enjoyed, but never to be understood by man."[57] Such a conclusion was a typical device for urging mankind to concentrate on the attainment of virtue and on the problems of human affairs rather than

---

[56] In chap. 3, p. 8, Logan argued that it is vain to fancy all may be spirit and that there is no such thing as body in the universe. See also his letter to Thomas Story (Nov. 15, 1737) in Penney, ed., *Correspondence of Logan and Story*, 64, where Logan rejected as an absurdity "Malebranche's notion of our seeing all things in God."

[57] Logan to Collinson, July 25, 1739. Logan was unstinting in his praise of Newton, yet at the same time he was continually finding petty reasons for censure. He failed to significantly criticize Newton's work, so instead he satisfied his high opinion of himself by frowning upon Newton's character and objecting to ludicrous peccadillos, such as that the third edition of the *Principia Mathematica* in 1726 contained a portrait of the great man as he was in his early forties rather than as he was in his eighties, Newton's age when the edition was published. See Logan to William Burnet, February 7, 1727, printed in Wolf, ed., *Logan's Library*, 349: "Scarce any man living has had a greater veneration for that surprising genius [Newton] . . . than myself." Logan then adds: "He is, however great, but a man."

on physical speculation, which was a widespread theme at the time. Yet Logan also accepted that there is an "avidity of knowledge implanted in the human mind, and these kinds of speculations are so far from being injurious that they rather improve, and raise the thoughts to contemplations that may prove truly profitable to such as are capable of them, as well as entertaining."

Chapter 3, on the intellect, was a necessary complement to Logan's empiricist beginning. If all knowledge begins with elementary sense data, one must then show how the process of transformation takes place that eventuates in the complex formulations and far reaches of the human mind. Yet extensive treatment of the subject has been rendered "needless," Logan believed, for Locke has "so judiciously and fully inquired into" it. Even so, if "The Duties of Man" is "to stand together," Logan said, he must consider the subject anew in his "own manner that the whole may appear of a piece" (chap. 3, p. 2r). This formal requirement was given some heat after Logan read early in 1736 Peter Browne's *Procedure, Extent and Limits of Human Understanding* (London, 1728), a work that sharply attacked Locke's theory of knowledge and therefore undermined the very basis of Logan's book. Logan's mission in chapter 3 became in good part that of refuting Browne.[58]

The issue between Browne and Logan may be simply stated. Both men (and Locke) accepted fully the Aristotelian and scholastic dictum that "we understand or know nothing but what is derived to us through our senses."[59] But Logan, like Locke, used this principle as a starting point only and went on to dilate on the "powers of the mind . . . to expand themselves afterwards to so vast an extent." The mind can form within itself "such infinite numbers of ideas and so very different from those first sensations," that to Logan it appeared "as if it were furnished with a capacity in it self by a little practicing on those simple ones to evolve other powers that were at first only virtually latent within it" (chap. 3, p. 7r). Occasionally this expansion of intellectual powers is illegitimate, which is particularly noticeable in metaphysics and sometimes in natural philosophy, when men speculate on the infinity of space and duration or other "vain pursuits," but Logan had no doubts that we can gain absolute knowledge in ethics without the aid of divine revelation. Browne, on the contrary, took the sensationalist or empiricist principle and "layes it *without any restriction or limitation* for the foundation of his discourse" (chap. 3, p. 6r) (Logan's italics), confining human understanding to material sensation alone and denying to men any reliable knowledge whatsoever of immaterial bodies, incorporeal spirits, or the abstractions of ethics. His goal was to protect divine revelation from being reduced to a demonstrable or a geometric science such as was proposed by the advocates of natural religion and naturalistic ethics. Logan's "Duties of Man," of course, fell into this despised category.

---

[58] Browne was Bishop of Cork. There is a deft critique of his thinking in Leslie Stephen's *History of English Thought in the Eighteenth Century* (New York, 1962; orig. publ. 1876), I, 94–100. The *Procedure* was closely and unfavorably reviewed in the journal *Present State of the Republick of Letters* of July and August 1728. I described the role of learned journals in keeping colonials informed of what was happening in the world of thought in Fiering, "The Transatlantic Republic of Letters: A Note on the Circulation of Learned Periodicals to Early Eighteenth-Century America," *William and Mary Quarterly*, 33, no. 4 (Oct. 1976), 642–60.

[59] Logan quotes the dictum thusly, chap. 2, p. 6.

Knowledge of God and of His attributes, according to Browne, can be acquired by analogy only, which gives us but a rough understanding and is itself only possible because of the faintest and remotest reflection of God's nature in the material world and in man. Our adherence to Christian religion and ethics must be by faith, Browne insisted, which by definition is exercised in the *absence* of adequate knowledge. Those who have endeavored to defend the duties of morality by "pretended metaphysical demonstration," Browne said, are guilty not only of "a palpable absurdity," but of having done "a great deal of hurt by furnishing the world with an handle for thinking that nothing in natural religion is to be regarded as strictly obligatory, further than that it is capable of such demonstrative proof." In addition, such a way of reasoning insinuates that natural religion, which is alleged to be demonstrable, is superior to revealed religion, which is capable only of probable evidence.[60]

Browne on the one side, and Locke and Logan on the other, disagreed fundamentally on the meaning of the term "idea," which ever since the publication of Locke's *Essay* had been subject to confusion in British thought. Browne insisted on restricting "idea" to mean the "sense impression" or "image" of an external object, derived through the sense organs. Given this definition, it followed that there could be no "ideas" of God or His attributes or of any non-material concepts. Locke, and Logan following him, had gotten away from this limitation by calling direct knowledge of one's own mental operations a form of ideas no less than external sense impressions. Moreover, Logan argued, common usage allows for the word "idea" to be substituted for "conception," "notion," and so on. "Is there any absurdity in that title of a book *An Inquiry into the Original of our Ideas of Beauty and Virtue*," Logan asked? And is it not equally proper to say, there is a pleasure in contemplating the "conception" of friendship or the "notion" of charity, "as to say the Ideas of them" (chap. 3, p. 2v)? An idea, Logan said, is any object in the mind, whether it be in the memory or the imagination, a reflection upon sense data, or a reflection upon a reflection. The main point was, that by recognizing direct knowledge of our own minds as primary data, the groundwork is laid for arguing that we have direct knowledge of some, at least, of the attributes of God and the abstractions of ethics. Man can know a little about God because he knows himself, who in his spiritual parts resembles God.[61]

In general, Logan emphasized the creative activity of the mind more than had Locke. Since the publication of the *Essay Concerning Human Understanding*, a number of philosophers had called attention to a deficiency in Locke's theory in this respect.[62] In any case, Bishop Browne's argument that the imagination stored sense impressions without any preceding activity of the mind was entirely

---

[60] *Republic of Letters*, August 1728, p. 125.

[61] "The Port-Royal Logic of 1662," by Antoine Arnauld and Pierre Nicole, known to virtually every educated person for fifty years after its publication (in either the French, the Latin, or the English edition), had already presented a broad definition of "idea," which included not only reflection upon our own inner experience, such as knowledge of "thinking" or "willing," but also conceptions of things known perfectly for which no mental image is possible, such as a thousand-sided figure.

[62] See, e.g., G. H. Leibniz, *New Essays concerning Human Understanding*, trans. Alfred G. Langley (New York, 1896), 276.

unacceptable to Logan. "Without an act of the mind in some degree," Logan said, "no idea can be lodged in us" (chap. 3, p. 4r). Logan particularly stressed the function of *attention*, which Locke had also briefly mentioned, in determining the strength of the images, and he portrayed the imagination as a creative rather than a passive faculty. Locke, as opposed to Malebranche, had hardly mentioned the active side of the imagination, Logan noted. There is a passive side to imagination, namely memory, when the imagination serves only as a storehouse of images waiting for recall, but the imagination taken actively, "which is truly the sense of the word . . . is very different[,] for this is the power of assembling images together, of ranging them at pleasure, heightening and enlarging them or lowering them[,] and throwing them into some series, not truly according to the real experiences of things, unless by accident but at the will of the disposer. . . . In a quickness of this consists what is called wit" (chap. 3, p. 5r).[63]

Logan's account of the operations of intellect also touched on the other traditional powers: apprehension, reasoning or inference, judgment, and will, but with little novelty. Given Logan's deep interest in and enjoyment of mathematics, it is perhaps worth mention that he recommended geometry and algebra above all as useful for training the judgment by accustoming the mind "to that sort of graduation and process" (chap. 3, p. 5v).

After disposing of Browne's exaggerated empiricism (and the fideism that followed from it), Logan could return to his essential message in describing man's intellectual faculties, which was that although man encounters insurmountable obstacles in gaining a profound knowledge of the physical world, he is well fitted, on the other hand, for perceiving moral truth. Like Locke, Logan returned again and again to the theme that man can only move so far from the foundation of his knowledge in sense perception, and he repudiated a purely rationalist approach in morals and religion. It "may appear shocking," Logan wrote, to those who "so highly exalt the powers of reason" and make it "an efflux of the deity and a participat[or] in some degree as it were of the divine nature," that our knowledge is dependent only on the primary materials of sensation. Yet from this human condition, man can learn both humility and caution. We must learn to "limit our inquiries and forbear carrying them into matters perfectly unfathomable by our very short line" (chap. 3, p. 6v). It is questionable, Logan asserted, that we "can be said to have any real knowledge at all of the world and nature, a thought that must undoubtedly depress our condition exceeding low. . . ." On the other hand, the situation is not all bleak, for in the things that "truly concern us" we can discover truth. The balance of man's intellectual capacities and incapacities reveal what "pursuits were intended for us, and what attainments, by being wrapt up in obscurity are denied us." Our facility at learning enough about the objects around us to make them useful to us, indicates that we should employ our time "on such chiefly as may truly

---

[63] The changing conception of the power of imagination has been excellently described by Ernest L. Tuveson, *The Imagination as a Means of Grace: Locke and the Aesthetics of Romanticism* (Berkeley, 1960). It is clear that Logan is writing after the publication of Addison's famous series in the *Spectator* on "The Pleasures of the Imagination." Hobbes as well as Malebranche was an important precursor of Addison, although in this area Locke did not borrow from Hobbes. See Clarence Thorpe, *The Aesthetic Theory of Thomas Hobbes* (New York, 1941, 1964).

render us happy" (chap. 3, p. 7r). Inevitably, Logan was leading up to the position that the proper study for man is the study of virtue: "That virtue only makes our Bliss below; and all our knowledge is, ourselves to know," in the words of Logan's favorite poet, Pope.

Beginning from simple ideas of sensible objects, the expansion of the mind, Logan suggested, is something like the metamorphosis of the silkworm from a small egg, which with nourishment of green leaves produces silk, grows wings, and so forth, no hint of which possibilities were evident in the tiny egg itself or the "contemptible little maggot" that came out of it. "We strike out conclusions so far transcending in degree those first materials we begin with, that they might seem almost of as different a species as vegetables are from some of the animal kind." We find opened to us and are enabled to enter, as it were, "a new kind of world of ideas, as of virtues, vices, modes, habits, relations, obligations, duties, merit, with divers others that cannot be directly produced by any species or simple idea of the senses" (chap. 3, p. 7v).

Following Hutcheson now, and not Locke, Logan pointed to the evidence that man has an involuntary susceptibility to viewing certain relations in the world in moral terms. Using an example similar to those in which Hutcheson had criticized Locke, Logan argued that when we see a person performing a "grateful or compassionate action" toward another, we receive from our sight "no other idea than those of the figure and motions of the person." Therefore, the gratitude or compassion of the action consists in an "idea" of an altogether different kind from those received by the sense of sight alone.

Implicit in his argument was the notion of the moral sense, or a faculty for perceiving moral relations as distinct from any other. The very same physical actions will be interpreted differently, Logan said, depending upon circumstances. If we see one man giving another a purse of money, and we are told it is robbers dividing their loot, our response will be altogether different than if we are told it is an act of charity from one good man to another (chap. 3, p. 7v). Thus, moral assessments are basic forms of meaning and not reducible to external sense data alone.[64] We have "very great reason to believe," Logan held, that our "abstract ideas of the relations of things, such as power, wisdom, goodness, duties, and the several virtues, vices, etc., though divers of them may originally have a very great

---

[64] Cf. Shaftesbury's *Inquiry*: "In a creature capable of forming general notions of things, not only the sensible things that offer themselves to the sense are the objects of the affections; but the very actions themselves, and the affections of pity, charity, kindness, justice, and so their contraries, being brought into the mind by reflection, become objects." Quoted in Ernest L. Tuveson, *The Imagination as a Means of Grace*, 53. As Tuveson points out, this was to go one step beyond Locke into the realm of moral conceptions, yet the development was an easy one. Tuveson also calls attention to the visual stress in Locke (see pp. 21–23, 73, and passim), which was the source of considerable misunderstanding concerning man's "knowledge" of values. The difference between the two scenes depicting the transfer of money lies in what the observer is told. The meaning comes from a framework of language and has ultimately a verbal foundation. The excessive visual stress of so much eighteenth-century moral thought, especially after Locke, was a profound bias that cannot be investigated here. Walter J. Ong's *The Presence of the Word* (New Haven, 1967) is an excellent prolegomena to the subject of the limitations of a one-sided visual orientation.

dependence on our sensations or affections; yet are in themselves as real as any other knowledge whatsoever" (chap. 3, p. 9v). The idea of a virtuous action may as easily and truly be abstracted from a concrete action as a number can be abstracted from things numbered, and this abstract idea may also be compared and related to other ideas.

When it came to belief in the fixity or definitiveness of moral concepts, Logan, Locke, and Hutcheson were once more in agreement. Locke had reasoned that since moral ideas are not themselves things in nature, which can be known only superficially, but are in fact definitions, it ought to be possible to define them so precisely and exhaustively that a kind of calculus could be brought to ethical questions. Though Locke and Hutcheson differed on the origin and nature of moral ideas, they agreed that they could be organized into an exact science, comparable to mathematics. The dream of a demonstrable science of ethics was not original with Locke, of course, since a number of writers in the seventeenth century had tried to geometrize philosophy in all its forms, most notably Spinoza in ethics. Logan was in fact one of the last of a string of moralists who were convinced that there could be a geometry or algebra of moral actions. Between Locke's time and the renewal of the concept in Bentham, the approach seems to have been largely abandoned.[65]

Logan's system for mathematicizing ethics was mostly an extension of Hutcheson's.[66] The ruling axiom or "the one universal standing equation throughout the universe eternally subsisting," according to Logan, is justice. On the basis of justice, labor must be recompensed by pay, public merit by public honor and gratitude, private merit by private gratitude, homage by protection, crime with punishment, and so on. Like Hutcheson, Logan attempted to figure in negative and positive factors based on motivation or intention. A good service done accidentally when the contrary was intended leads to a deduction from its value. When a good act is done through "real and sincere benevolence, its value . . . is augmented in duplicate ratio." In the same manner are crimes to be considered. After relating a group of similar principles, Logan concluded: "And thus generally all the conduct of mankind in civil life may be estimated and equated and morality be as fully and clearly demonstrated, as those sciences called the mathematics" (chap. 3, p. 10r). Peter Browne was wrong, Logan added, "to set mathematical and moral certainty at so great a distance."

Logan was aware of some of the difficulties a truly demonstrable ethics must overcome, but he minimized them. He observed that in mathematics the ideas of the terms, being perfectly defined, are distinct and clear, but the process of deduction and computation itself "frequently becomes very perplexed and intricate,"

---

[65] There is a good brief discussion of this subject in W. von Leyden, *Seventeenth-Century Metaphysics* (1968), 204–206. See also, Louis I. Bredvold, "The Invention of the Ethical Calculus," in Richard Foster Jones, *The Seventeenth Century: Studies in the History of English Thought and Literature from Bacon to Pope* (Palo Alto, CA: Stanford University Press, 1951), 165–80.

[66] Logan used the 1729 or 3rd edition of Hutcheson's *Inquiry*, which still retained the ethical computations. In the 1738 or 4th edition, Hutcheson withdrew the whole section, which Logan was not aware of.

whereas in morals the calculation themselves are not complex, but rather "short, plain and easie"; it is the ideas themselves "for want of that care" used in mathematics to find strict definitions that often prove to be obscure and uncertain. But "Why may not we conceive as clear and distinct an idea of a kind action as of a circle?" Logan asked. There exist in morals "self-evident truths" little different from the axioms in geometry. Such truths, Logan said, "prove themselves to the understanding by such plain common sense as all men agree in[,] and as there can be no principles more clear to prove them by[,] therefore they admit of no other demonstration than their own inherent evidence" (chap. 3, p. 10r). Once the terms and axioms are strictly defined the procedure in ethics would be the same as in mathematics, "for in all reasoning on mathematical, moral[,] or any other subjects the process and conduct of the mind is just the same" (chap. 3, p. 10v).

In Francis Hutcheson's moral arithmetic, five axioms were posited, which were to serve as a universal canon to compute the morality of any actions. The factors in the axioms were each given symbolic notations to speed computation. M = moment (or amount) of good produced; A = ability of the agent; B = benevolent intentions; I = the self-interest of the agent in the results of his actions. The benevolence of the agent is found by subtracting from the moment of good the amount of personal interest involved, that is when interest and virtue concur; when virtue is disadvantageous, i.e., against self-interest, then the self-interest is added to the benevolent intentions. The formula for the latter looks like this:

$$B = \frac{M + I}{A}$$

Yet, how can one weigh and measure intentions or degrees of benevolence? Although there may be agreement on some universal axioms of morals—e.g., each man should receive his due—it is impossible to arrive at a consensus on the precise application of the terms in any given case. It might be enough to dismiss Logan's *folie geometrique* as an instance of cultural lag in America if we did not know that a thinker as sophisticated as Francis Hutcheson was still toying with the idea in the third edition of his *Inquiry*, published in 1729.[67] The explanation may be found, perhaps, in the moral uncertainty of the age, which I have already adverted to. When the ground of ethical truth seems to be shifting below one's feet, or left solely to faith and revelation such as Peter Browne proposed, men will grasp at any system that promises some degree of certitude. It is "a very great wrong to our understanding and no less an abuse on mankind to set moral certainty at such a distance or indeed at any at all from geometrical," Logan wrote in reply to Browne.

---

[67] Laurence Sterne ridiculed Hutcheson's computations, though the author of *A Sentimental Journey* had in common with Hutcheson the emphasis on moral sensibility: "Hutcheson, in his philosophic treatise on beauty, harmony and order, plus's and minus's you to heaven or hell, by algebraic equations—so that none but an expert mathematician can even be able to settle his accounts with St. Peter—and perhaps St. Matthew, who had been an officer in the customs, must be called in to audit them." Quoted in William R. Scott, *Francis Hutcheson: His Life, Teaching and Position in the History of Philosophy* (Cambridge, 1900), 32.

## Of the Passions

Logan's self-criticism notwithstanding, his fourth chapter, on the passions and affections, was a remarkable accomplishment for a colonial British American in the
first half of the eighteenth century. Although he did not develop an entirely consistent or original theory, the chapter is well-informed and comprehensive. The im-
broglio over the anatomical "seat of the passions," despite its importance to Logan,
does not diminish the worth of the chapter as a whole.

Logan opened the chapter with the by-then familiar recognition of the central
importance of a theory of the passions to moral philosophy, for on the regulation and
adjustment of the motions of the passions, he said, "principally depends all our happiness in life."[68] The stoic approach, which makes man "only a creature of the brain,"
is severely dismissed. The stoics "declared war" against the passions, Logan wrote,
which sometimes had good effect and produced virtuous men, "yet at the same time
[the stoics'] great ignorance of humane nature appears by it" (chap. 4, p. 1r).

Logan found most of the early theories deficient, such as the scholastic distinction between irascible and concupiscible passions, and the typical classifica-
tory schemes, nearly all of which, according to Logan, among other things left out
pride and shame. Only with the work of Descartes, who introduced a new system
of his own, was "the whole Peripatetic philosophy [brought] into discredit." Descartes wrote on the passions "much more justly and accurately than anyone who
had gone before him" (chap. 4, p. 2r). However, he made the error, Logan noted,
of denying that the seat of the passions is in the heart.[69] Indeed, Logan believed,
"all those [authors] the writer has seen . . . place them in the soul, in the brain, in
the judgment, or in the imagination, etc." (chap. 4, p. 2r).[70] Logan's conclusion in
this regard is rather strange, since the traditional view, reinforced by much figura-
tive language, tended to assign the passions to the heart rather than to the brain,
although there was enormous confusion in distinguishing vasomotor responses
from types of mental consciousness and in relating them to each other.[71]

---

[68] "Duties of Man," chap. 4, p. 1.

[69] Descartes argued for the pineal gland.

[70] Logan mentioned specifically, in addition to Descartes, Jean Baptiste Duhamel, and Thomas
Willis.

[71] There is a brief discussion of the history of theories of the seat of the passions in H. N. Gardiner,
et al., *Feeling and Emotion* (1937), 132–37. Hobbes, for one, had placed great emphasis on the
role of the heart in the expressing of emotions. Logan explicitly drew on the tradition that sup-
ported his view while at the same time claiming some uniqueness for himself. He wrote in chap. 4,
p. 3 of the "Duties": "The ancients were so sensible of the affections and operations of the heart
that they made it the seat of wisdom of thought and understanding. In the Scriptures very many
expressions occur to this purpose. . . . " Other evidence from Greek and Latin literature is cited.
"And though they mistook who assigned thought to the heart, yet in other respects they certainly
judged well, in allowing it so great a power and command, and so large an interest in the whole
of humane conduct." Logan also cited the evidence from common language—"heavy heart," "light
heart," etc. A Harvard College commencement thesis from 1689 asserted: "Passiones sedem suam
primiariam in Cerebra hebent." The passions have their primary seat in the brain. This claim was
probably based on Antoine LeGrand's *Logick*, 333, which argued explicitly that the passions are
seated in the brain, not the heart.

Logan's insistence that the heart is the seat of the passions was based primarily on the argument that the passions are "vastly different from ideas," and therefore cannot belong to the brain. An intellectual truth, he said, is universal: $2 \times 2 = 4$ is the same for everyone and can be taught to all. This is characteristic of any clear and distinct idea. But how "plant courage in the place of fear?" for example. At best, in order to establish something of this kind it is necessary to make use of practice and habit (chap. 4, p. 3r). Moreover, Logan continued, actions of the mind in the brain, when the mind is employed solely in reflecting on its own ideas, are in themselves calm, quiet, and regular, whereas always the effects of passion show themselves in some impulse or motion. "It is from hence sufficiently evident, that our ideas, which in truth are no other than our knowledge, and these passions are in their nature wholly different and intirely distinct. Though it is no less certain that they are each so constituted as very strongly to affect each other."

Ironically, the rigidity of Logan's distinction depended upon an excessively narrow definition of "idea," the very flaw he detected in Peter Browne's work. Certainly, the passions include visceral responses, but subjective conscious experience is also part of them so that mind and body are inseparably coordinated. Logan's argument might be thought of as an eighteenth-century anticipation of the famous James–Lange theory, which posited that bodily changes follow *directly* from perception of the stimulating object and precede the mental feeling that we call the emotion or the passion. The feeling is a consequence of the autonomic bodily changes. The two major objections to this theory would apply as well to Logan's argument about the centrality of the heart in emotional experience: first, the very same hormonal and vasomotor changes seem to be characteristic of a number of passions, which suggests that the differentiating factor is the mind, not the body; second, people with severed spinal cords report a full range of affectional states. In other words, sensations in the mind, whether called "ideas" or not, are fundamental in the experience of the passions, perhaps even more so than visceral changes.

Logan was still more the victim of the literary and religious tradition when he asserted that not only do the transient passions spring from the heart but also "the more durable inclinations and dispositions and those from which men generally take their moral characters, as when we say one man is good, merciful, generous, grateful, another haughty, cruel, revengeful" (chap. 4, p. 4r). Many seventeenth-century theorists of the passions distinguished between two levels of affection in this manner. Hutcheson also spoke of the enduring, calm, and sedate "affections" in contrast to the violent and temporary "passions." Figuratively it makes sense to say, in Logan's words, "the abilities of the head, the rectitude of the heart, are vastly different." But on what basis can it be assumed that the core of temperament or personality literally resides in the heart? And, indeed, in this instance Logan did not even attempt to give the idea a physiological or anatomical explanation.

We have already noted Logan's analysis of the difference between an "idea" and a "passion" as one proof of his theory that the passions do not exist in the mind essentially. He also introduced several other arguments. First, of course, there was the alleged anatomical evidence, which we have already looked at, except to mention that this was one more application of the premise Logan had laid down in his first chapter, that "nothing in nature can move or act otherwise than by, and agreeably to, the powers it is in its original intention invested with."[72] All the parts of the body, Logan reasoned, can perform only the motions for which they are fitted—we can bend our finger to the palm but not back to the wrist. The heart is no different. Its anatomy suggests its end or purpose. "All our passions must be original powers from nature planted in the heart, nor ought we to search any further for the cause of their production." The cause, in other words, is providential. Logan brought into this proof, too, his control group, namely animals, whose nerve structure in relation to the heart, he believed, is significantly different (chap. 4, p. 9v).[73]

Second, Logan adduced the involuntariness of the passions as proof of their independence of the mind, which is characterized by reason and volition. "We find our hearts are susceptible of love, hatred, fear, or anger; yet we cannot by our utmost endeavours . . . love, hate, fear, or be angry, by an act of volition." Even less, Logan observed, can we love an object that appears hateful to us, hate what appears lovely, fear what is desirable, or be angry with what pleases us.[74] Here Logan was clearly borrowing from Hutcheson, who had earlier pointed to the apparent determined or involuntary character of the passions as proof of their providential autonomy. Like Hutcheson, Logan described an autonomous mechanism connecting the object with the specific passion that is raised. Every object, he said, has its "respective and correspondent passion," which rises "by nature's direction . . . without any act of our will or reason" (chap. 4, p. 5).

On this basis Logan took issue with Locke, whom he correctly interpreted as a psychological hedonist in the sense that in Bk. 2, chap. 20, secs. 3–5 of his *Essay*, Locke spoke as though the passion of love, for example, let us say to one's children or friends, is an idea that arises in the mind following upon reflection on the pleasure we feel in their happiness or their very being. One of the implications of this theory is that all of the passions are assumed to be merely modifications of pleasure and pain in the organism and reducible to forms of pleasure and pain.[75] It also seemed to follow from Locke's brief statement that we love what gives us pleasure, rather than the other way around, namely that we get pleasure from what we love. Under Locke's reckoning, Logan said, our passions become "merely subservient to our pursuits of pleasure, and declining of pain." If a man were asked why he loved his children, it is unlikely, Logan said, that he would answer that he loved them because they gave him pleasure. His only reply could be that he loved

---

[72] As restated in "Duties," chap. 4, p. 5.

[73] Logan cited Cumberland as an authority, as follows: "There is in men a notable plexus in the intercostal nerves, from whence divers branches are sent down to the heart communicating with the diaphragm none of which are to be found in brutes; from whence he [Cumberland] deduces some considerable argument to the advantage of our species." But even Cumberland did not carry the deductions far enough, Logan said. Cumberland himself relied on Thomas Hillis, it should be noted. See Cumberland, *Treatise of the Laws of Nature*, trans. Maxwell, chap. 2, secs. 26–27.

[74] For discussion of the background of this distinction, see Fiering, *Moral Philosophy at Seventeenth-Century Harvard*, chap. 3, "Will and Intellect." See also, Fiering, *Understanding Rosenstock-Huessy* (Eugene, OR: Wipf and Stock, 2022), chap. 10.

[75] Benjamin Franklin, in what can only be considered a sophomoric work, his *Dissertation on Liberty and Necessity, Pleasure and Pain* (1725), took Locke's theory to extremes. See the Epilogue, below.

them because they were his children, that it was natural for him to do so, and that he could not avoid it. "In such cases . . . Nature has made a sure provision, without leaving it to the work of reflection or consideration" (chap. 4, p. 5). Our passions, in other words, are purposeful mechanisms that provide the conditions for pleasures and pains. As Hutcheson had described it, the various "senses" other than the external, that is, the moral, the public, the aesthetic, or whatever, give rise to specific sensations that in turn lead to inclinations that when satisfied bring pleasure or when frustrated bring pain. In accordance with this theory, pleasure and pain are rarely, if ever, the motives for action. They are the by-products of action. Moreover, when put in such a context, pleasure and pain lose their subjectivity. Rather than being merely arbitrary and unpredictable personal experiences without any connection to the moral universe, pleasure and pain become themselves indicators of divine will.[76]

"Good is the proper object of the heart," Logan wrote. When something appears good to the mind, the affection rises to it. The good in relation to us is that which "gives or procures us pleasure, immediate or mediate," but the pleasure must be "consistent with the end of our formation, which in respect to us, is our own happiness." Happiness as an end, however, is also not simply a personal or subjective measure. Happiness, Logan said, is no more than the continuation of pleasure, and pleasure is a sensation of the "suitableness of an object to the sense, appetite, affection, faculty or power in us, fitted in our formation to be moved or affected by it." Thus, pleasures and pains in relation to the organism are programmed in accordance with higher purposes. Moreover, all pleasures are not equal. Their value is to be estimated in accordance with the faculty affected by them, and so also must the good be valued that is the cause of the pleasure. In other words, the higher the faculty or the sense, the higher the good. The pleasures of the moral sense take precedence over the pleasures of the external senses, for example. This psychological system is, of course, subject to error in that our affections or inclinations may be wrongly directed. But the source of the error is in the mind, in our opinions, or in the imagination. "The heart itself never mistakes in its own first motions." On the other hand, "raised affections," by which Logan meant, presumably, violent passions, can sway the understanding and lead to wrong determinations. Mistakes arise from the mind failing to duly examine the true nature of the subject (chap. 4, pp. 12–13). It was on the basis of this analysis that Logan, like Shaftesbury and Hutcheson, could dismiss the evidence of "unnatural" and immoral practices in the world as having no bearing on the integrity and reliability of the heart as a judge of what is right for man. The proper function of desire is to "put into stronger motion" the inclination of the heart to obtain the proposed good (chap. 4, p. 15).

---

[76] The most complete argument for the moral role of pleasure and pain as part of divine design appears in chapters 2 and 3 of Bishop Butler's *Analogy of Religion*, ed. W. E. Gladstone (1736), 52–53: "The foreseen pleasures and pains belonging to the passions, were intended, in general, to induce mankind to act in such and such manners. . . . [God] has appointed satisfaction and delight to be the consequence of our acting in one manner, and pain and uneasiness of our acting in another, and of our not acting at all." This proves, according to Butler, that we are under God's government "in the same sense, as we are under the government of civil magistrates."

Logan was also unconvinced by Locke's assertion that a passion is an *idea* that follows reflection upon the experience of pleasure or pain. Locke had said outrightly in the *Essay* (II, xx, 17) that although the passions are usually accompanied by specific bodily effects, such changes in the body "do not make a necessary part of the idea of each passion." At least some passions, in Locke's view, were clearly located in the head. In the scholastic tradition there had long been a distinction between passions of the mind and passions of the body, but Logan interpreted Locke to mean that the passions "turn on reflection." It is not altogether certain that this is what Locke intended, but Logan was convinced, in any case, that Locke had propounded an intellectualist theory of the passions. Locke may have meant no more than that consciousness is a necessary part of emotion. "It is sometimes indeed a matter of deep reflection and consideration," Logan wrote, "to know whether an object is good or not, but this inquiry has no immediate regard to the affection, for the moment, the very instant, that it appears good in the imagination . . . the affection as instantaneously rises to it," that is, without any intellectual mediation. In other words, the affections respond involuntarily to the apparent good or evil of the objects encountered.

Logan accepted that emotional responses begin with sensation, and to that extent the brain is immediately involved. The heart has no sense organs. But the transfer through the sensory nerves to the heart is virtually instantaneous, and, as we have noted, Logan attempted to substantiate this theory with anatomical evidence following Thomas Willis and Cumberland. The anatomical evidence was so precise, Logan believed, that it revealed the exact status and role the passions were designed to have in the human moral economy: the nerve connections show that the passions are properly involuntary, but also designed to be subjected to some control by the rational faculties. The head, of course, must be the ultimate ruler. "Scarce a thought ever rises in the mind, but as suddenly an intermixture of some affection from the heart is found . . . cooperating with it," which is as it should be. But "too often, the affection or passion bears the command and becomes the principal director" (chap. 4, p. 11r). Logan was confident that the "supreme faculty" of reason, which it was intended by God should govern, could with no great difficulty "distinguish" the officious or exorbitant influences of passion in any given case, and thus keep them in their proper channel.

Yet, as we noted with regard to his discussion of self-love, Logan was not naive about the effects of passion in subverting rational decision. Any new idea, he observed, instantaneously evokes some liking or disliking, some pleasure or uneasiness, even "before the understanding or judgment can be at all employed to weigh or consider it." Logan detected a propensity in men to take sides even when there is neither knowledge nor interest in a case, as one might do witnessing a fight between two strangers. The factions in Renaissance Italian politics came to his mind as an example of the extreme irrationality in such divisions. "Even from very trifles[,] or what has no solid foundation in nature[,] have such currents of the affections been raised, like large rivers that frequently rise from almost imperceptible drains in marshy places, . . . [and] engaged vast numbers in factions and parties most pernicious in their consequences" (chap. 4, p. 11r).

By and large, however, Logan was more impressed by the positive contributions of the passions to the enhancement of virtue than by their power to self-deceive.

Pride, he recognized, could be one of the "most dangerous passions," but its intended use is to lead us to improve ourselves and to attain "such qualifications as may recommend us to the esteem of others" (chap. 4, p. 15r). Honor and ambition derive from it, both of which may be conducive to good, which makes pride one of the most excellent ingredients or qualities in the "whole human composition." Emulation, too, as Hesiod said (he called it "contention"), was given from heaven to men as a blessing, Logan noted. It is clear that Logan was almost completely emancipated from the seventeenth-century essentially religious concern with the purity of intentions. The passions, when they are functioning in accordance with nature (or the divine intention), assist men to reach rationally desirable ends and that is all that matters.

The balance of Logan's discussion of the passions and affections is mainly concerned with an analysis of particular passions and their uses. His aim was to demonstrate in detail what Henry More had similarly undertaken in the previous century, that "all our appetites[,] sensations[,] affections[,] and passions have manifestly been given us for ends directly tending to our support, pleasure or happiness" (chap. 4, p. 13r). There is no need here to recount his treatment of each passion, though it should be noted once more that, to my knowledge, there was no other similarly comprehensive and systematic treatment by an American in the colonial period. Love, joy, grief, hope, despair, fear, compassion, envy, anger, shame, pride, and others, Logan briefly analyzed.

The one major innovation, or, at least, deviation from the usual components of such a discussion, is Logan's suggestion that "natural conscience" is a passion rather than a function of intellect. "All must own that when conscience accuses, anguish is felt in the heart as sensibly as any other of its emotions," and this feeling, Logan believed, is distinct from grief, fear, and all other emotions (chap. 4, p. 17v). Grief always has an exterior cause, Logan noted, and fear is different because it is aroused in relation only to some future evil. Logan accepted the term "remorse," however, as more or less synonymous with his meaning, so long as this emotion was not confused with grief or fear. His description is none too clear, but Logan's point seems to be that there is a highly specific emotion that arises in connection with moral trespasses that is not reducible to any other emotions.

The intellectual element in conscience remains, however, as Logan acknowledged. "The object of conscience is right and wrong in human actions as reason dictates or determines." This characteristic of conscience would seem to be a limitation on the functions of a moral sense. But Logan was in fact striving for some kind of synthesis of the intellectual and the sentimental schools. The "passion" of conscience also functions in a positive role, Logan suggested, by "watching over every other operation, every motion and action of the other passions," and "joyn[ing] with the best." It unites most closely with love, when love is "raised to the highest and most perfect object the mind is capable of conceiving." One thinks here of Henry More's "boniform faculty" and of various Puritan interpretations of holy zeal. Logan gave as an example the courage of religious martyrs, where indeed there is the firmest possible union of intellectual belief with emotional reinforcement. The conscience of martyrs is a passion, or it is nothing. This reference to religious martyrdom surely drew on Logan's inherited memories of the persecutions suffered by the Society of Friends in the seventeenth century. But the "Duties of

Man As They May Be Deduced from Nature," as its title indicates, contains almost no discussion of the relation of moral philosophy to religious teaching. Only in a remarkable letter to the Quaker missionary Thomas Story, written on July 12, 1736, do we get a hint of Logan's own problems of conscience that arose in connection with the book. In this letter he was more candid than anywhere else about the extent to which he had come over to the benevolist position and about the difficulty of relating his philosophy to the Christian dispensation.[77]

Logan told Story that when he first began his investigations his goal was to present the evidence "without any view to any profession of religion whatever." Yet it is apparent that Logan never expected to end up excluding any need for divine grace. It came as a surprise to him that when he was through, "nature" had absorbed the whole system. "The Creator at first furnished man with strong natural inclinations to lead him into the practice of all the social virtues." These inclinations are called natural, Logan said, because they are universally implanted in the species. It is true that by a perverse use of his free will, man became corrupted, "yet there are still sufficient remains of that primitive splendor . . . which, if duly cultivated, may yet lead him to happiness." The proof of this survival is not "reason," Logan told Story, though that is the common way of talking and the faculty of reason may be a "great guide." But "I am fully persuaded," Logan wrote to Story, "that without the concurrence, and even the leading of the affections, reason contributes very little to virtue; it distinguishes, and when not too much biased decides, but it rarely incites; this is the work of the heart, and, I am convinced of it, was so intended in our formation." This conclusion left a big question, however, as Logan knew. If this be natural, Logan asked Story, "where is the divinity of it otherwise than as it is the work of the Creator"?[78]

Logan was faced with the same dilemma that Jonathan Edwards also had to grapple with. The sentimentalist persuasion was deeply convincing. Where then does one find the influence of special grace? If one assumes the heart of man is rotten, the effect of religion is to bring about a change of heart. But once assume that the heart is itself providentially directed to worthy social ends by "nature" alone, then the unique effects of religious influence are forced to become super-refined if they are to be recognized at all.

We do not have Story's reply, but it is apparent from Logan's next letter that Story had pressed him on his religious commitments. For on November 15, 1737, Logan composed an extensive defense of his procedures. From his youth, he said, he had been unable to acquiesce in any sort of knowledge without knowing also "the first and deepest principles" on which that knowledge rests. "It has been and is my rule and method to investigate the truth and reality of things abstracted from all prejudices whatever, with the most intense care and application." And although he believed it improper to publish freely all one's thoughts, yet what

---

[77] Logan had sent Story a copy of his 1736 *Charge from the Bench to the Grand Inquest* where many of the ideas we have already seen were summarized. The nature of conscience was extensively debated among seventeenth-century Puritans. See Fiering, *Moral Philosophy at Seventeenth-Century Harvard*, passim.

[78] Penney, ed., *Logan and Story*, 57.

one does publish must be that which one believes is true. But after stating all this, Logan did declare to Story his conviction that in the end the highest attainments in morality require divine assistance. When the passions and affections are duly regulated by reason, and directed by "a good understanding," morality is perfected, and this is the true foundation of all "social duties," that is, presumably, civic virtue. But when there is "joyned to this a true sense of our dependence on the supreme and divine Author of all things, a constant contemplation of his wisdom and goodness, and a sincere love springing from thence, influencing us by the bent of affection, to observe and practice . . . the same good order that he has established throughout his creation . . . this is true religion and holiness." Divine influence, then, can crank up the affections still more than is typical of their natural bent, and this is the highest virtue. Defending specifically his ranging of natural conscience amongst the passions, Logan told Story that he was persuaded that by this theory he was doing a great "service to virtue and true religion; for I have there left full room for all superior influences."[79] The very notion of "leaving room" for God betrays how far Logan had moved from the foundation of his Quaker faith. Transitions of this sort went on in thousands of souls in the eighteenth century.

There could be no doubt, as Story sensed, that Logan had sharply confined the area of divine influence, for it turns out he was much more fearful of religious enthusiasm than of the dangers of naturalism. There are "well meaning friends," he pointed out to Story, referring to his fellow Quakers, who "imagine" that all the thoughts that are suggested to them from a sense of divine love when they are preaching "are the dictates of the Spirit." On "some very peculiar occasions," Logan said, God may reveal a particular truth, but this is not the common way, "for it is certain that the motions of the heart and [the] thoughts of the head are very different." A man that has a strong passion for a woman will find "a great many warm thoughts" spring up in his mind, which are raised and influenced by his affections. And anger, hatred, and other passions will bring about thoughts. Similarly, "when the heart is touched with divine love, pious thoughts will be suggested," but these for the most part partake of "the natural temper and disposition of the speaker as well as indicating his natural abilities or weakness."[80] Logan here was contending with the same problem that prompted Jonathan Edwards in 1746 to publish his *Treatise concerning Religious Affections*, how to distinguish natural emotion from the special effects of divine grace.

Logan was aware in 1737 of the evangelical stirrings in the colonies called by historians the Great Awakening. His predispositions, like those of Samuel Johnson of Connecticut, were opposed to the Awakening, even though he adhered to a sentimentalist moral psychology, as Johnson did not. It is perhaps not unfair to speculate that men with long practice in rational approaches to the world will be distrustful and at least reticent when confronted with what appears to be uncritical

---

[79] Penney, ed., *Logan and Story*, 62–63.

[80] Penney, ed., *Logan and Story*, 66.

religious emotion. In December 1740 Logan gave Peter Collinson the following description of the great evangelical preacher George Whitefield:

> Probably you may by the time this comes to thy hand (if ever) have heard as much of Whitefield as I can tell thee, for by his Journalls[,] Letters on All Occasions, etc. which are industriously printed here nobody can long be a stranger to any thing that relates to him[;] and in his life work by himself and printed here as it doubtless will soon be there he has been scandalously plain. All that I have to say of him is, that by good language[,] a better utter-ance[,] and an engaging voice and manner he gained much at first on most sorts of people, but on his falling foul of Archbishop Tillotson and that most unexceptionable author of the Whole Duty of Man etc. the more judicious fell from him: Yet he still gained on the multitude insomuch that they have put forward [for him] in Philadelphia a brick building for him to preach in of 100 [feet] in length and 70 [feet] in breadth in which though not yet covered he a great many times preached when last here about 2 or 3 weeks ago. It must be confessed his preaching has a good effect in reclaiming many disso-lute people, but from his countenancing so very much the most hot headed Presbyterians and those of them principally who had been accounted by the more sober, little better than madmen, he and they have actually driven div-ers into despair and some into perfect madness. In short it is apprehended by the more judicious that the whole will end in confusion[,] to the great prejudice of the cause of virtue and solid religion. His doctrine wholly turn-ing on the danger of good works without such degree of sanctifying faith as comes up to his gage.

Logan's stress on the "judicious" should be noted. Whitefield offended many by saying that Archbishop Tillotson, whose popularity in the colonies, north and south, was unrivaled, had no more religion than Mahomet.[81]

Like Jonathan Edwards later (especially in his *Nature of True Virtue*), under the influence of the benevolists Logan had conceded so much to the good effects of natural passions that religious influences, the effects of the Holy Spirit, inevitably became highly specialized. "I am strong of opinion and firmly believe," Logan told Story, that there is "something divine attends mankind, exerting itself in that part of him that, in my discourse on the affections, I have called natural conscience." But what are the effects of this attendance? "When ardent desires are raised in [the] heart to know the will of God," divine grace, independently of our will, "puri-fies, animates, and strengthens" them. We know that Story was not entirely satis-fied with this merely ancillary role for divine grace.[82]

---

[81] On Archbishop Tillotson's unrivaled popularity in British America, see Fiering, "The First American Enlightenment: Tillotson, Leverett, and Philosophical Anglicanism," *New England Quarterly* (September 1981, 307–44). *The Whole Duty of Man*, a devotional work attributed to Richard Allestree, was in the library of every literate Christian in Britain and America.

[82] See Logan's letter to Story of November 19, 1738, in which he proposed to close the discussion by conceding that the gift of grace "is the only source of true happiness attainable in this life." Penney, ed., *Logan and Story*, 69.

## The Foundation of Virtue

In the spring of 1736, Logan composed the fifth chapter of his study in ethics, which was the last he ever completed. It was designed to tackle two major questions: 1) Whether man is led to moral good by nature or only by laws or religions, and 2) What foundation can be discovered in nature for the distinction between moral good and evil? In preparation for this task Logan read in particular—and "considered them almost every page"—Hutcheson's first two books (that is, the *Inquiry* and the *Essay on the Passions*) and John Balguy's *The Foundation of Moral Goodness* (1728–1729), a critique of Hutcheson.[83] The juxtaposition is significant, for it becomes clear in chapter 5 that Logan had hopes of effecting a synthesis, or at least a compromise, between the sentimentalist and intellectualist schools, although this plan may have arisen only after his reading of Balguy and possibly did not occur to him until after he had finished the first four chapters of his manuscript.[84]

At the beginning of chapter 5 of the "Duties" Logan surveyed the state of the question as it presented itself to him in 1736. He recognized three general schools: In my terminology, the Hobbesian; the intellectualist or rationalist; and the benevolist. With regard to the first, Logan was mainly interested in demonstrating how much Hobbes was an anomaly. Before Hobbes wrote, Logan observed, the theories inherited from the ancient world almost universally assumed that man was made for society, and in the early seventeenth century Grotius, for one, believed there was a natural disposition to benevolence in children. Bishop Sharrock, Richard Cumberland, James Tyrell, Pufendorf, Samuel Clarke, and Shaftesbury, among others, also opposed Hobbes.[85]

---

[83] The surviving Logan manuscripts include 12 octavo pages of notes on Hutcheson's *Inquiry* and additional pages with excerpts from Hutcheson's *Essay on the Passions* and from Balguy. On July 25, 1739, Logan told Collinson: "I have . . . considered them [i.e., Hutcheson's books] almost every page, for their subject being the same with that of my 5th chapter, i.e., moral good, on which in a long discourse of at least 50 pages in folio I examined every hypothesis and consequently his, though scarcely properly his . . . for his notion concerning beauty is taken from Crousaz [i.e., J. P. de Crousaz, *Traité du Beau* (Amsterdam, 1715; 2nd ed. 1724)] and that of virtue from Shaftesbury. I also considered that of Balgey [*sic*] who writes himself in the title of churchman and is the author of 2 little tracts on the foundation of moral good, wrote with much good manners in opposition to Hutchinson's [*sic*] notion, who founds virtue on an inward principle which he after Shaftesbury calls the moral sense, while Balgey asserts it to [be] reason[.]" Logan had probably read Hutcheson's *Inquiry* once before in about 1730.

[84] It seems probable that Logan read Balguy for the first time in the spring of 1736, and this resulted in some alteration of his position concerning the place of reason in moral judgment. For although Logan knew Samuel Clarke and Wollaston well, and Balguy did not significantly add to their arguments, Balguy was responding directly to Hutcheson, whereas the earlier men wrote before Hutcheson.

[85] James Tyrrell, *A Brief Disquisition of the Law of Nature, According to the Principles and Method laid down in the Rev. Dr . Cumberland's . . . Latin Treatise on that Subject. . .* (1692; 2nd ed., 1701) was highly influential as the best English presentation of Cumberland before John Maxwell's translation in 1727.

The opposition to Hobbes divided into the two other schools: 1) that which holds that both moral judgments and the obligation to moral conduct "turns wholly on reason," and 2) that which "asserts a natural bent in the soul of man to good from implanted affections and inclinations that lead him to benevolence and a concern for the public good, for which end a moral sense is given." Although these schools later became sharply distinguished, Logan observed that earlier writers, such as Grotius and Pufendorf, made use of both opinions. Cumberland also drew from both positions, Logan believed, although he seemed in Logan's opinion to be most in harmony with the moral sense school.

Logan gave particular attention to John Selden, author of *De Jure Naturali & Gentium* (1665?), for he believed that Selden was the first to distinguish the "ratiocinative faculty," such as is the subject of Locke's *Essay*, from the other kind of reason, which is "derived from or established by the command[,] authority[,] and indication of the parent of nature, the supreme being." Selden went on to show that it is from the second kind of reason only that the *jus naturale* is derived, whereas the first, also known as the "understanding," remains undirected by any superior authority or "ingrafted principle," and can be no criterion by which to judge good and evil. Samuel Clarke, Wollaston, and the other rationalists obviously have in mind only the second kind of reason, whereas Shaftesbury and Hutcheon concentrate on the inadequacies of the first. Part of the problem after Selden had been the confusion in the meaning of "reason." Selden himself, Logan believed, like Cumberland, meant by this second kind of reason nothing less than the moral sense of Shaftesbury and Hutcheson; so, he, too, is representative of the seventeenth-century synthetic view on which Logan hoped to build (chap. 5, p. 13).[86]

Reason is "a great and noble gift of heaven," Logan wrote, with many capabilities for observing distinctions in the world and in action and conduct. "It can often discover and trace up effects to their causes, discern and contemplate the beauty[,] regularity[,] and order that shines out in all parts of the creation that have relation to us and our faculties," and from this viewpoint, reason can tell us how we ought "proportionably to regulate our own inward conduct and that of all our actions." But we must not carry reason's claims higher than is "proper and genuine" (chap. 5, pp. 10–11).

In addition to the powers of reason, there is no doubt, Logan continued, that "we are so framed as to be affected with pleasure from beauty" (chap. 5, p. 16). The exactness of the analogy between aesthetic and moral perceptions was unquestioned by Logan. The same people who deny "all sentiments of nature in relation to virtue or moral good, likewise assert that there is no positive or real beauty in things, but the whole depends on fancy or humour" (chap. 5, p. 19). Logan believed, however, that there are universal criteria in both cases, whatever the contrary evidence. The variety of tastes that may be found in the world proves only "the prevalency of custom in some cases over nature." In order to get to the truly natural dictates and sentiments, Logan argued, it would be necessary to observe the first appearance of them in children. Logan was convinced that Africans and

---

[86] Logan borrowed from Cumberland almost word for word in his discussion of Selden.

Chinese naturally prefer Caucasian facial features to their own. "Were any of those people . . . to give their judgment of the beauty of a flower, of a tree, a bird, a horse or other animal, or ranges of trees, or of anything where there are no particular customs or prejudices to warp them, can we imagine they would differ much, if anything from us in opinion about them?" (chap. 5, p. 21).

Locke's assertion that there is no natural standard of moral good, and his citation in the *Essay* of anthropological evidence indicating that even parental cherishing and care of their children is not universal, was especially painful to the Philadelphia moralist. What does this evidence from all around the world prove, Logan asked? Suicide and fasting also regularly occur in various societies, but this fact does not lead us to deny a universal instinct for self-preservation and for food. Indeed, Logan wrote, "there is no law, no affection, no appetite, no principle, whatsoever, innate or acquired, so radicated in the heart of man, but that by a fixt resolution he may conquer it—for he was formed an accountable creature, and therefore had also superior to all those appetites and principles freedom of will" (chap. 5, pp. 81–83). The truth of this statement could also be used to support an argument for man's inherent malleability, indeed, his irrepressible urge to transcend all "natural" limitations, as much as for an argument for human uniformity, but Logan was hypnotized by the eighteenth-century quest for immutable laws in nature and society. He was certainly nowhere near ready to welcome the power of "fixt resolution" as the awesome key to human emancipation from the weight of the past no less than it may be the basis of perverse customs.

The perception of beauty does not depend on an *understanding* of the laws of proportion and harmony or in any way on reason. The contemplation or view of beautiful objects, even those that have no special relation to us, will "in many instances diffuse a joy, very sensibly perceived in the heart from that contemplation only." Beauty, therefore, is capable not only of raising a localized sensation of pleasure, but "it extends it self much further by exciting the passions of joy or gladness." These emotions, Logan noted, are in fact an "inseparable concomitant of every pleasure not disapproved by reason or the judgment." And just as the external sense first discovers and distinguishes beauty without the aid of the understanding, so also, without the direction of reason, the pleasure affects the heart. Music is a prime example of this process (chap. 5, pp. 24–30). The diffused pleasure and the discrimination that is characteristic of the exercise of man's aesthetic sensibilities is, then, a psychological model for understanding his other non-rational powers. Logan referred back to his fourth chapter for examples of how the affections, too, have pre-ordained pleasures and pains. But the pleasure of perceiving beauty he considered to be a function of external sense rather than of the affections.[87]

---

[87] Cf. Hutcheson, *Inquiry*, ed. McReynolds, 8: "It is of no consequence whether we call these ideas of beauty and harmony perceptions of the external senses of seeing and hearing or not. I should rather chuse to call our power of perceiving these ideas, an internal sense, were it only for the convenience of distinguishing them from other sensations of seeing and hearing, which men may have without perception of beauty and harmony."

Even our appetites, which are given for necessary support, have "super-added a further concomitant pleasure" as an inducement. Thus, eating, child care, sleep, and so on, are not left to rational deduction, however plain their necessity may be, or left to impassive instinct. Instead, we take gratification from these activities, and pleasure is attached to what must be done for survival in any case (chap. 5, pp. 62–63).

The next level—and here Logan seems to be rearranging Hutcheson slightly—is that of the intellectual pleasures, which are the "purest, most perfect[,] and consequently the most worthy of a rational being" (chap. 5, p. 31). These arise from three kinds of knowledge: mathematical, physical, and moral. In his *Inquiry*, Hutcheson had spoken of the "beauty of theorems" at considerable length, attempting to show how the same general principles of proportion and harmony, or of uniformity amidst variety, evoke pleasurable sensations in us from many different classes of phenomena. Logan is generally obedient to Hutcheson's treatment, citing the pleasure afforded by a study of the properties of the circle and various mathematical laws, the proportions and balance of ideas in literature, and the beauty and order of the forms that reign through the whole of nature. "We clearly find," he wrote, "that the most sensible delight we receive even from those intellectual pleasures that have been mentioned, turns much more on the affections and a conformity with the principles carefully implanted in us by nature in our original composition, than on any other art or attainment whatsoever" (chap. 5, p. 44). In short, it is not rational cultivation that is the key to these responses, but innate mechanisms, and the approval or disapproval that is implicit in these responses is not inference, or deduction, but pure affection.

From these premises Logan was prepared to move to a more precise definition of the role of the natural affections in leading men to virtue. First, however, the question of the foundation of virtue or moral good had to be addressed, and here is where Hutcheson was found deficient, and Samuel Clarke, Wollaston, and Balguy have their way. One may justly wonder, Logan wrote, that a person of "so clear an understanding in other respects as [Hutcheson]," could attack the sentiments of "two illustrious modern authors justly received by the world with the highest approbation[,] Dr. S. Clarke and W. Wollaston" (chap. 5, p. 55). Despite these encomiums, however, Logan's own argumentation suggests that it was Balguy's cogent reply to Hutcheson that was decisive in his own thinking.

Consider the intellectual processes of the ideal natural man, Logan said, the primitive child of nature, in effect. He would not "overindulge" his appetites for fear of weakening his reason, which should be his "sovereign part" and "sole rule and guide in the whole conduct of life." From observing the harmony, order, and "mutual subordination" of the parts of the natural world this primitive would be (as Shaftesbury showed) strongly led "to reduce all his affections[,] passions[,] and inward emotions to the like equability and harmony within himself, conformably as near as might be to that exterior order" observable in the creation (chap. 5, pp. 51–52). The cosmos as depicted by Shaftesbury, where "order, proportion, fitness and congruity in the relations of things universally reign," serves as an image of the ideal interior order. The outcome of this inward shaping can only be "the calmest serenity and most solid peace of mind," and consequently the truest happiness. This happiness and contentment, the result of conformity to nature, which is the old stoic ideal, is the only conceivable end for which a power of infinite wisdom and goodness could have prepared man.

Natural reason will also lead an uncorrupted man to recognize the fundamental axioms of natural law: that he is but one individual in his species; that he is formed for society (here Logan referred to the arguments in his first chapter); that he is equal with all other persons in nature, all of whom have appetites like his own, and "the same title to happiness" with himself. He will see the value of cooperation. He "cannot fail of seeing . . . that he ought in all cases to do by others, as he would desire they should do by him," which is a rule "sufficiently extensive to ground all the mutual or relative duties of life on." The cardinal virtue of justice follows from these axioms, as the other classical virtues of courage, temperance, and prudence follow from imitation of the restraints, self-sacrifice, and order visible in the creation. In a more abstracted sense, justice may be defined as the "observing of the relative fitnesses in the nature of things, and applying each to the other" (chap. 5, pp. 54–55). The term "fitnesses" immediately suggests the influence of Samuel Clarke, Wollaston, and Balguy.

Logan's final synthesis was undoubtedly suggested by Balguy. The English clergyman writing in 1728 did not question that God has instilled in man benevolent affections toward others, and that these affections were given us in order to "engage, assist and quicken us in a course of virtuous actions."[88] But these affections are only auxiliaries, Balguy said; they cannot be the foundation of the idea of virtue. Virtue, or the moral good, must have a rational, immutable basis, such as $2 + 2 = 4$. Hutcheson was correctly revealed by Balguy to be a theological voluntarist who would be willing to accept that God, had He so desired, could have planted in man a negative response to justice. But this is to leave the moral law completely arbitrary. God must be absolutely good, and He must have had a good *reason* for the moral order such as it is, a reason which must be accessible to human reason. "It is no more in the power of the Deity to make rational beings approve of ingratitude, perfidiousness, etc., than it is in His power to make them conclude, that a part of any thing is equal to the whole."[89] The truths of morals, like any other truths, are subject to rational tests to which even God is subject.

It followed from Hutcheson's dubious principles, Balguy pointed out, that if God had not framed our nature with social propensities and benevolent instincts, that we would be altogether incapable of virtue, and "notwithstanding intelligence, reason, and liberty, it would have been out of our power to perform one action in any degree morally good." Given the supposition that men had been formed destitute of natural affections, and lacking particularly in kind instincts toward benefactors, would gratitude then have been absolutely out of our power, Balguy asked? "Might we not nevertheless, by the help of reason and reflection, discover ourselves to be under obligations, and that we ought to return good offices or thanks, according to our abilities?" Or supposing man void of natural compassion, as well as benevolence: "Might we not possibly be induced to attempt the relief of a person in distress, merely from the *reason* of the thing, and the *rectitude* of the

---

[88] Raphael, ed., *British Moralists*, para. 437.

[89] Ibid., para. 444.

action? Might we not, by considering the nature of the case, and circumstances of the sufferer, perceive some fitness, some reasonableness in an act of succour? Might not some such maxim as that of doing as we would be done unto, offer itself to our minds, and prevail with us to stretch out a helping hand upon such an occasion?"[90] These rhetorical questions were the heart of the rationalist argument: Human understanding is sufficient to determine man's moral duty in every case, and the foundation of the rightness or rectitude of conduct rests ultimately on considerations of reason.

In arguing that the nature of *right* is based on reason, not arbitrary divine fiat, and that a good action has its own inner logic which is reducible to "self-evident" propositions (Balguy used the word "self-evident"), the rationalists seemed to be on solid ground vis-a-vis Hutcheson. Where Balguy stumbled, however, in Logan's perception, was where he had also to show that reason was a *sufficient* incentive or inducement to virtuous action. In mediating between the sentimentalists and the intellectualists, Logan was no Hume, and he missed much of the subtlety in the problem. Logan was not equipped, in other words, to catch all of the shadings of language in Balguy's small book that enabled the author to slide quietly from morally neutral concepts like "assent" to such characteristically moral terms as "obligation" and "approval." But Logan did recognize that Balguy was much less convincing when he discoursed on the "motives, inducements, or *exciting reasons* for the choice of virtue," than he was when he treated the "*justifying reasons of our approbation* of it."[91]

Virtue was nearly correctly defined by Balguy, Logan maintained, as the "conformity of our moral actions with the reason of things" (chap. 5, p. 48). And Logan defended man's capacity to know the fitnesses of moral relations just as he knows the fitnesses of certain natural relations. We see immediately that a cube is unsuitable for rolling down an incline just as we recognize according to the rule of justice that it is wrong to break a promise or arbitrarily to deprive a rightful owner of his property. But for man's happiness on earth there is more to the story.

"It has been fully proved," Logan argued, "that to act virtuously is to act agreeably with reason or the nature of things in the several relations we and they bear to each other. But were the whole left there, virtue would consist in the study of these relations; and he who had gained the highest attainments in that knowledge might have the best title to the character of a virtuous man" (chap. 5, pp. 59–60). Is it possible that God has "so little befriended the principle of all his works on this earth" as to leave man with no other guide to virtue but "dim reason"? That faculty is the portion of only a small number of people and during their years of discretion. "Very few proofs [can] be found," Logan said (speaking from the vantage point of the cultivated American gentleman) "of any great influence that reason has upon the general mass of mankind." Yet however weak men's heads are, their appetites and passions seldom fail of being sufficiently strong, and "miserable would be their condition if they had no other monitor near them than their glimmering spark of reason, or their memory perhaps equally weak, to bind them to the discharge of

---

[90] Ibid., para. 439.

[91] Ibid., para. 453.

their respective duties" (chap. 5, pp. 64–65). A wise and good God would never have given men free will had he also not endowed them with instincts to compensate for the weakness of their reason.

Logan then reiterated the essential principle of sentimentalist ethics. Reason merely enables us to compare ideas and to observe their agreement and disagreement. It is "no principle of action in itself." Without the intervention of passions and affections, which are "the only springs of action in all human creatures," men would be motionless and the determinations of reason of very little use. Logan's synthesis is now obvious, if it was not before: virtue lies in the union of the affections with the appropriate moral ideas. The affections rise to the truths of morality, embrace them, and pleasure is diffused through the whole soul. "This is the great rule the Author of Nature has prescribed in his whole works" (chap. 5, p. 67). As the eye or the mind from its sensations discovers a beauty, and is "delighted with it in outward objects," or the ear yet more so with harmony, so the mind "no less plainly discovers and is sensible to the beauty of virtuous actions, and all are equally founded on the reason of things[,] on order and proportions." Logan credited Shaftesbury among others with formulating the same idea, as well as Plato and Cicero (chap. 5, p. 68).

There is implanted in the human soul, Logan wrote, a just sense of the interior beauty of actions, no less than of the beauty of exterior objects. "The affections have their respective springs and keys which when properly touched are exerted and the whole soul is affected by them" (chap. 5, p. 75). Thus, men are moved to virtuous conduct. "As wind and oars are to a ship or galley," so are the affections, "not only to virtue, but to our whole conduct in life." And as the pilot is to the ship or the driver to the chariot, so is the function of reason in the soul "in some measure but not in all respects or universally" (chap. 5, p. 79). The last qualification was necessary because Logan was a convinced believer in primitive or innocent goodhearted men (such as Fielding presented in *Tom Jones* a few years later), who are "so happily formed by nature in their composition, and their virtue has so far excelled in a native probity, modesty, and the whole chorus almost of the other virtues that they may without much danger be trusted to their own funds in themselves without further institution or direction" (chap. 5, p. 79). In other words, there may exist a degree of primitive virtue that may not require the guidance of reason, although this is the exception. The classic instance of this type in American literature is Billy Budd. Usually, reason is a needed guide.

It may be concluded then, Logan argued, that both those who contend for virtue being founded on reason and those who would ascribe it to moral sense are in the right for part of the way, but both also fall short of the whole truth insofar as they would exclude or derogate those propositions advanced by the other. Reason is the ultimate criterion of the determination of moral objects or ends; moral sensations and affections are the necessary incentives to moral conduct. Logan's final definition read: human virtue is "a conformity of our affections to the reason of things as founded in the general system of the universe" (chap. 5, p. 80).

It would be an unduly harsh judgment to condemn Logan's culminating synthesis as vacuous and abstract. For at the relatively superficial level at which he was philosophizing, the outcome was satisfactory. Viewing the problem from a distance, i.e., outside of the center of discussion in London and Edinburgh, and without real immersion in the formulation of the crucial issues, the instincts of a good-willed man are normally to create a paper synthesis. Both sides to the debate appeared to have strong points. The trick is merely to unite what is most prominently correct from each, leaving aside the disturbing questions, such as to what extent the defects of each position undermine, not just partially, but nearly totally, their respective arguments. A more critical approach might begin with the assumption that both sides had largely cancelled each other out, and from there attempt to rethink the problem, borrowing bits and pieces as necessary, but never moving unexamined blocks of thought en masse. The comparison is unfair, yet one need read only a few pages of Hume's *An Inquiry concerning the Principles of Morals* (1751), which addressed itself in large part to exactly the question of "how far either reason or sentiment enters into all decisions of praise or censure," to discover the insufficiencies not so much of Logan's conclusions as of his treatment.

Logan's response to this great problem in moral philosophy at mid-century was, nevertheless, highly representative of middle-level thinking. At almost the same time Logan was writing the "Duties of Man," a minister in Scotland, William Jameson, published *An Essay on Virtue and Harmony, wherein A Reconciliation of the various Accounts of Moral Obligation is Attempted* (Edinburgh, 1744). Like Logan, Jameson saw a "friendly correspondence of the instinctive and rational schemes." The two together, that is, the "indispensable natural obligation to the system of moral offices which is perceived by reason," and the "pleasant relish of approbation of them that is felt by the . . . moral sense," reinforce each other in demonstrating that the "frame of our nature" is essentially adapted to the performance of our duties. Moreover, Jameson suggested, these two ingredients of virtue are "mutually subservient," and the one "supplies the other's defects." If both sides to the question would avoid dogmatism, Jameson said, they might discover that their schemes "may not be at bottom so directly opposite as at first view they may seem." Each of them may have "a good title to be taken (at least their most capital parts) into one great plan." Jameson's solution was exactly like Logan's: "Our *moral sense* feels those things to be good, which *reason* discovers to be fit and preferable."[92] Jameson did not ask, nor did Logan, by what standard reason declares this or that end to be "preferable." If they had asked themselves this question, the answer could only have been: the fit and the congruous is preferable. If pushed still further, Logan, like Balguy, would have relied on the self-evidence of reason's perception of moral relations. In response to criticism in this area Balguy wrote: "For the reality of these relations [i.e., fitness and unfitness, agreement and disagreement, etc.], every man must be referred to his own perceptions, since they admit of no other proof."[93]

If, on the other hand, the pressure was exerted on the other half of the synthesis, and the reliability and uniformity of the moral affections brought into question, Logan would have taken refuge in the susceptibility of man's good nature to corruption and perversion. In matters of ethics, man does not have determining

---

[92] William Jameson, *An Essay on Virtue and Harmony* (Edinburgh, 1744), 269–77.

[93] Raphael, ed., *British Moralists*, para. 459.

instincts, as the brutes have for all their purposes in life. God has provided man with inducements and inclinations only. His freedom of choice or of will remains a problem, as well as being an opportunity for virtue. Logan's sixth chapter was intended to be a discourse on the will. It was here that the aberrations of nature could have been analyzed. Since the chapter was barely begun it would be reckless even to surmise what Logan would have said.

Two problems in particular associated with the will stood out as having maximum bearing on moral philosophy. The freedom of the will was one of them, since it was almost universally believed that moral accountability depended upon freedom of choice in some sense. Secondly, there was the question of discovering the basis of errant choice, so that the presence of vice in a world designed by a good God could be explained. In neither of these cases do we have from Logan adequate commentaries. With regard to the first, we know only that Logan insisted, in the conventional fashion, that man is not a machine, and that he has freedom equivalent to his accountability before God and man.[94] With regard to the second, Logan never got far enough in his chapter on the will to take up in detail the personal sources of vice or turpitude. We know only that he found Locke's discussion exceptionable, and indeed Locke's comments in the *Essay* are the focal point of the few pages of Logan's chapter 6 that were written (or at least have survived).

"The deeper we enter into the consideration of our will the more we shall find ourselves engaged in difficulties that perhaps will ever remain insoluble and inextricable," Logan recognized (chap. 6, p. 1). He was unable to agree with either of Locke's formulations concerning the propellant of willing: that which appeared in the first edition of the *Essay*—the will follows the judgment in choosing the greatest apparent good in every case—or that which appeared in all subsequent editions—the uneasiness of desire determines the will. Men often neglect what reason suggests is the preferable choice, Logan believed, nor are they always moved by preceding uneasiness. Either one of these motives may be counted as efficacious in particular cases, but neither one of them can be generalized as the sole motive behind acts of choice. Logan apparently was of the opinion that we are subject to spontaneous "inclinations" that have no antecedent cause, either in the reason or in the affections (chap. 6, p. 1).

Logan was particularly opposed to Locke's second formulation of the psychology of willing, that pain or uneasiness is the precondition of all desire, and that desire gives rise to acts of will. Logan's critique of this argument interestingly included among its targets Benjamin Franklin's youthful folly, his *Dissertation on Liberty and Necessity* (1725), a connection I take up in the Epilogue. Logan's principal objection applied both to Locke and to Franklin's *Dissertation*, namely, that this thesis about motivation conflicted with what is known or believed of God's goodness. Logan's optimism refused to accept that pain is natural, except when it leads us to care for our bodies against death and dissolution. Pain, he said, is not part of the institution of nature, "which puts us on all methods of avoiding it,"

---

[94] "Duties of Man," chap. 6, p. 1. Subsequent references to chapter 6 of the manuscript will be in parentheses in the text.

except in the two cases of parturition and dentition. These two instances "it must be owned are not to be accounted for," but surely, Logan continued, "no man was ever so absurd as to imagine that nature, which has shewn deep design in the formation of every minutest part of us, intended that we should be ever ailing in our bodies and ever applying accurate expression of how God makes use of pain in the world." Thus, if by "uneasiness" is meant bodily pain, the thesis is questionable. "Disquiet of mind," however, Logan accepted as a more plausible source of desire, although here, too, he said, there are exceptions. Contrary to Locke's argument, Logan argued that man was not intended to be "continually subjected to a flux or series of succeeding uneasinesses," but rather for a state of pleasure. Nature undoubtedly designed the human species "as sound and healthy as other animals." Look at the pleasurable condition of childhood, Logan suggested, and in a fine, revealing passage he adumbrated what has become a familiar criticism of some theories of twentieth-century psychology that hold that all action springs from a sense of deficiency or pain in the organism. Consider "a clear summer morning," Logan wrote, when gaiety "overspreads the whole face of nature," the birds chirping and the viewer in good health. "Such a person with the same continued gaiety sets about every act his duty calls him to, with pleasure he sees it proceed under his hands and when the time for refection calls him with an appetite just raised to a height to give a pleasure in the gratification he returns to it, not sensible of the least uneasiness but with a serenity of joy diffused o're all. And this," Logan said, "is truly the condition of life designed for us by the supreme Lord of Nature" (chap. 6, p. 6).

Logan's main point was that we often act without sensations of uneasiness, even in the case of strong appetites. The signals are neutral, in other words. Locke's thesis is absurd in itself, Logan argued, for if the uneasiness is worth removing, and if it can be removed by volition alone, "it is done instantaneously by an act of the will." The need is answered in most cases, Logan apparently believed, before there is even a sensation of pain. I may think in "my judgement it is better for me to put on my shoes than goe all day in my slippers, and according to this determination[,] without any manner of uneasiness[,] I will to have my shoes on" (chap. 6, pp. 4–5). This would be an example of the judgment influencing desire, although Logan did not make this point.[95]

One has the impression that Logan, had he completed his sixth chapter, would have argued for the so-called "liberty of indifference," or the self-starting will. He would have maintained that it is the potential independence of the will from both judgment and affections (which on the whole steer men rightly) that causes most of the trouble in the world, and yet this independence is necessary if men are to be fully responsible creatures. This might be called the naive view of the will.

---

[95] Logan used this same example also to show that will and desire were not so far apart as Locke had put them, for, he said, continuing the illustration, to desire that one's servant put the shoes on for him is no different than willing to put them on himself. In order to distinguish will and desire, Locke had called attention to the difference in usage: we "will" only what pertains to our own actions, but "desire" the occurrence of things outside of ourselves. Cf. Locke, *Essay*, XX, xxi, 30. I review at length the elements of the eighteenth-century discussion of the will in *Jonathan Edwards's Moral Thought and Its British Context*, chap. 6, "Morality and Determinism."

From the one other relevant composition of Logan's, his *Charge . . . from the Bench to the Grand Inquest* of 1736, which was designed to be a summary of his thinking about moral philosophy and was printed by Franklin, with a subsequent edition in London, we can derive only a few further hints. Confronted with blatant criminality as it is manifested in arraignments before the court, Logan was compelled to comment to some extent on the nature of vice and moral evil. But even in the *Charge* Logan's tone is predominately enthusiastically optimistic—it is full of Shaftesburian-type eloquence on the beauty and order of nature and on man's innate goodness—although there are also dark references to the possibility of "some inward taint, some wrong bias or perversion of the inclinations" that accounts for criminal conduct.[96] In the glory of creation, "man, only man," a wonderfully framed creature with extraordinary capacities, "this creature man, I say, our own species man, exorbitates and runs into disorder and wild confusion, of which he *alone* is the only instance throughout the whole *creation*" (chap. 6, p. 9). God could not have intended this contradiction to the harmony of the Whole, which suggests that there has been "some great degeneracy, some grievous deflexion from our original rectitude, owing to a violent abuse of that great gift, free will," which was bestowed with the faculty of reason (chap. 6, p. 9). This vague reference to original sin is the extent of Logan's glance at the problem of the origins of moral evil. He offers thereafter only the briefest analysis of the psychology of vice and sin. Those appetites and passions whose chief objects are bodily pleasures, "by our degeneracy not only became inordinate, but got the mastery, and usurped dominion," and the "calmer and milder affections were deadened and stifled, and even the powers of reason seduced, and gradually wrought over to joyn with its enemies, those irregular passions" (chap. 6, pp. 10–11). The problem here, of course, is that only the evils of sensuality are accounted for, but not the evils of the spirit. Most of Logan's address, as I have indicated, is devoted to demonstrating that the toll of original degeneracy has been so slight, that "humane nature is not so altogether sunk and depraved" or so "extinguished or defaced" that "those nobler impressions inclining us to the love of truth, of justice, of benevolence, and the other virtues" still retain sufficient force "to exert themselves in every breast, where any tolerable degree of innocence has been yet preserved" (chap. 6, p. 11).

Logan's grand jury, his auditors, must have faced the task ahead of them with good will and cheerfulness. One might guess that few presentments were made that year in Philadelphia. On the other hand, by painting so eloquently the glories and beauties of virtue, Logan made all crime appear outrageously

---

[96] *Charge to the Grand Inquest*, 4–5. Logan sent Thomas Story a copy of the *Charge* in 1736 and commented in a letter dated April 12 of that year: "It is fit I should inform thee that in forming that discourse I framed not nor proposed to my self any manner of hypothesis; I had nothing further in view than at my quitting that Station [of Chief Justice] to say something usefully instructive and edifying to the people; and though I was to be in court . . . on the 2nd day before noon, I had not the preceding first day morning so much as resolved what the particular subject should be, which I mention only to shew how far I was from all previous intention of advancing any singular opinions." Logan's *Charge* of 1736 was first printed in Philadelphia by Franklin and reprinted in 1737 in London. Though apparently composed in one day, it is a creditable work.

horrid and unnatural, so far from the true nature of things as to be almost beyond understanding.

> When we once entertain a true notion of that great and primary law, by which the whole universe is supported, *viz.* Justice, and of the reasonableness of doing every one, as we would they should in like circumstances do by us; we should utterly abhor the thought of offering any wrong to our neighbour. To attempt to deprive him of his right, either in his estate or possession, or, what is more dear to all good men, their credit and reputation, would become detestable; and those villainous practices of calumny and scandal, that some make so free with, but are truly the scum of corrupted souls, thrown out by the acrid ferment of malice, with its foundation in falshood, would appear as odiously black, as the hellish source it springs from. And then far would it be from human thoughts to perpetrate such heinous outrages, as the depriving of our fellow creatures, partakers of all the rights of nature equally with ourselves, of that by which alone they can enjoy them, *viz.* their lives; the crime for which all nations have appointed the like punishment. (18)

Logan's strategy as a moralist was like Addison's, Hutcheson's, and others, namely, to avoid so far denigrating human nature that there is no model or standard of goodness left to adhere to. There is no other way of explaining how a man so worldly, so seasoned in the fracas and self-interest of provincial and court politics, could have looked upon society so ingenuously. Faced with what seemed to some to be the inevitability of moral anarchy following the decay of religious leadership, Logan was among those who found grounds for hope in God's benefactions to man outside of the Christian dispensation. With Hutcheson, who must surely be seen as Logan's ultimate inspiration, Logan believed that if men could only be made fully conscious of their natural endowments that are supportive of virtue, conscious to the extent that they will favor and encourage these endowments, the outcome would be a reign of peace and tranquility both in the outward world and in the inner mind.[97]

---

[97] Hutcheson's profound influence on Logan can be measured by a comparison of Logan's 1723 *Charge Delivered from the Bench to the Grand-Jury* with the 1736 *Charge . . . to the Grand Inquest.* In the 1723 *Charge* one finds scarcely anything that could not have been written fifty years earlier.

# Epilogue: Logan and Benjamin Franklin

The most famous "moralist" in early British America is Benjamin Franklin, both then and now. Note, "moralist," not moral philosopher. After a brief experiment with the genre, Franklin rejected philosophical intricacy and disputation, but he was a staunch promoter of the benefits of moral virtue. Virtue was the only road to personal happiness, he maintained, and at the same time a sound basis for service to mankind as a whole, a mission that Franklin both preached and practiced. He intended to write a self-help book on the "art" of attaining virtue, famously described in his classic autobiography.[98]

The total corpus of literature about Franklin is huge, and the output never ceases. He is endlessly entertaining and interesting. My purpose in bringing Franklin into this essay on Logan is only to round out in a few pages the interwoven relationship between the two men in the specific area of moral philosophy, not to add generally to all that has already been said about Franklin. Bringing in Franklin adds a bit more context to Logan's major effort in moral philosophy, and it is Logan who is our focus.

In a recent book about Franklin, we hear: "In matters of intellect, Franklin's debts to James Logan were immense. . . . If the Franklin of the early 1730s needed a mentor, Logan was ideal." The author of these words, Nick Bunker, argues, too, that "the influence of James Logan, the freethinking Quaker, was far more significant in the shaping of Franklin's career than the cultural legacy the latter received from New England Calvinism."[99] We have to presume that Bunker meant, when he referred to Logan's shaping of Franklin's "career," Franklin's "thought," not his career, since neither Logan nor "New England Calvinism" was much of a formative influence on Franklin's career. Moreover, it is a wild mischaracterization to refer to Logan as in any way "freethinking" and a considerable stretch to describe Franklin's intellectual debt to Logan as "immense." All that said, generalized a little, the claim about Logan's influence is a good starting point. Logan's biographer, Frederick Tolles, commented that many of Franklin's moral admonitions and practices were as much derived from the Quaker environment in Philadelphia as from his upbringing in early eighteenth-century Puritan Boston.[100] The altruistic

---

[98] See Norman Fiering, "Benjamin Franklin and the Way to Virtue," *American Quarterly*, XXX, 2 (Summer, 1978).

[99] Nick Bunker, *Young Benjamin Franklin: The Birth of Ingenuity* (New York: Knopf, 2018), 254–59.

[100] Tolles, "Quaker Business Mentors: The Philadelphia Merchants," in Esmond Wright, ed., *Benjamin Franklin: A Profile* (New York: Hill and Wang, 1970), 7–18. The relationship between Franklin and Logan, despite the age difference and political differences, is nicely outlined in Tolles's biography of Logan.

strain evident in Franklin, aiming at the good of mankind, was present in New England Puritanism in the seventeenth century, exemplified in such a work as the English pastor Richard Baxter's *How to Do Good to Many: or, the Publick Good is the Christian's Life* (London, 1682), but it paled beside the requirement of personal spiritual regeneration.

Franklin himself testified to the influence of his Boston upbringing on a life devoted to public service in a nostalgic letter he sent, late in life, to Cotton Mather's son, Samuel Mather. Writing from Passy, outside of Paris, on May 12, 1784, Franklin credited Cotton Mather with shaping his career. "When I was a boy," he told Samuel Mather,

> I met with a book, entitled "Essays to do Good," which I think was written by your father. . . . [This book, Cotton Mather's *Bonifacius, or Essays to Do Good*] gave me such a turn of thinking, as to have an influence on my conduct through life; for I have always set a greater value on the character of a doer of good, than on any other kind of reputation; and if I have been, as you seem to think, a useful citizen, the public owes the advantage of it to that book.[101]

In Franklin's youth Cotton Mather was definitely a major presence in Boston because of his broad learning and extraordinarily prolific output in print, but there is little reason to think that he had a major influence on Franklin, who in this letter to his son was simply being courteous after Samuel had complimented him. In fact, Cotton Mather and the rebellious young Franklin were mostly at odds until Mather's death in 1728. Whatever the case, the model of the useful citizen was in the air in the first half of the eighteenth century in both Massachusetts and Pennsylvania.

Leaving aside the question of influence, despite a thirty-two-year disparity in their ages and a disparity, too, in social class, Logan and Franklin became friends and mutual admirers. Logan was among the most learned men in the colonies with a scholar's library of some 3,000 rare volumes, a lodestone to which Franklin was drawn, whereas Franklin was manifestly brilliant and inventive, a man of infinite curiosity constantly generating practical ideas.[102] Logan recognized his unmistakable genius and gift for leadership and enjoyed his company. The assiduous Franklin biographer J. A. Leo Lemay asserted that "Logan was evidently Franklin's favorite intellectual conversationalist in the Philadelphia area."[103] They not only talked about books, they cooperated also in achieving some political goals, among them the need to prepare Philadelphia's defenses against an attack from the French by sea, an urgent concern on which Franklin took the lead in the community. The doctrinaire opposition by pacifist Quakers to preparation even for defensive war was mitigated by Logan's support of Franklin on the question. His having held

---

[101] Franklin's letter to Samuel Mather is easily found online on the website of the Massachusetts Historical Society. David Levin's introduction in the modern reprint is informative: Cotton Mather, *Bonifacius, An Essay upon the Good,* ed. David Levin (Cambridge, MA, 1966).

[102] Edwin Wolf 2nd, *The Library of James Logan of Philadelphia, 1674–1751* (Philadelphia, 1974).

[103] J. A. Leo Lemay, *The Life of Benjamin Franklin,* vol. 2 (Philadelphia, 2006), 310.

several major offices in the colony, including mayor of Philadelphia and chief justice of Pennsylvania, as well as being the spokesman for the Penn family and a
prosperous fur merchant, the Quaker Logan's opinions carried unmatched weight
in the community.[104] In 1750, after they had been of assistance to each other for
a number of years on various practical matters in the colony, Logan, then in his
mid-seventies, shared his appreciation of Franklin in a letter to Peter Collinson
in England. Logan mentioned first Franklin's initiative in organizing militias for
defense of the region and his role as "Sole Author of two Lotteries that raised above
Six thousand pounds of our Money to pay for the Charge of Batteries [i.e., cannon]
on the River. . . ." "In Short," Logan continued,

> he is an excellent yet a humble man, and carried himself a Musket among
> the Common Soldiers. He is also now putting forward an Academy for the
> improvement of Youth, for which he [has] already got Subscriptions for
> above five hundred pounds per annum for five years. . . . But I must here add
> that thou hast Seen my Tully of old Age of which he printed a thousand. . . .[105]

"Tully of old Age" refers to Cicero's *Cato Major de Senectute*, which Logan had
translated into English as a birthday gift to his aging friend Isaac Norris. Franklin
offered to typeset and print the book for Logan, lavishing attention on it, with the
result that the finished product, published in 1744, is one of the finest examples of
eighteenth-century American typography. The contents justified Franklin's care,
for Logan adorned his translation with scores of interesting, learned footnotes
that take up half or more of the entire text of 159 pages! Every proper noun of
persons, places, and historical events in Cicero's essay was explicated by Logan.
In this collaborative work, both men displayed distinctive and refined skills. Earlier Franklin had published *Cato's Moral Distichs, Englished in Couplets* (1735)
from a translation made by Logan for the use of his daughters. This short work,
pervasive in Latin grammar schools, was a made up of proverbs, admonitions,
and the like, and another indication of the concern for moral education that the
two men shared.

Logan and Franklin became acquainted, it seems, in 1731 when Franklin was
promoting the founding of a lending library in Philadelphia, the beginnings of what
was to develop into the present-day Library Company. The population of the city at
the time was about 5,000, and men of intellect found each other. Logan's help was
sought in choosing what books to acquire for the library. Among their commonal-
ities, both Logan and Franklin were self-made in a sense, although Franklin as a
printer was a mere "mechanic" in the social demography of the time while Logan
was the secretary and representative in the colony of the proprietary Penn family.
Logan's father, however, was only a schoolmaster, in Scotland and then in Ireland,
and Logan himself became a schoolmaster, never attending a university. His father

---

[104] Logan wrote to Franklin (Dec. 3, 1747): "Ever since I have had the power of thinking, I have
clearly seen that government without arms is an inconsistency." *Papers*, 3, 219–20.

[105] Feb. 28, 1750. *Papers*, 3, 469–72. In a P.S. to his letter to Collinson regarding Franklin,
Logan added: "Pray do not imagine that I overdoe it in my Character of BF for I am rather short
in it. . . ." Logan then adds more details of Franklin's contributions.

gave him a strong foundation in classics and other subjects, and Logan did the rest to train himself as a scholar in a number of areas, including modern languages and mathematics and botany.[106] That William Penn recognized his talent and hired him should be no surprise.

Franklin, too, was self-educated after grammar school, although he was not the beneficiary of parental support for a life of learning. On the contrary, his father balked at the expense of sending him to nearby Harvard, casting Franklin in the role of tradesman instead, which Franklin deeply resented at the time. In his teens, when by right he should have been in college, Franklin salved his pain by making a virtue of his deprivation, ridiculing in print in precocious essays in his brother's newspaper the snobbery and superficiality of supposed academic achievement. Franklin's persona in these essays, a Mrs. Silence Dogood, reports on a dream she had, in which

> Every Peasant, who had wherewithal, was preparing to send one of his Children at least to this famous Place [Harvard], and in this Case most of them consulted their own Purses instead of their Children's Capacities: So that I observed, a great many, yea, the most part of those who were traveling thither, were little better than Dunces and Blockheads.[107]

Entrance to the college required "Riches" above all, Franklin (as Mrs. Dogood) went on, while within the institution "Idleness" and "Ignorance" prevailed. "Latin, Greek, Hebrew, &c . . . seldom or never unvail'd their Faces here, and then to few or none, tho' most of those who have in this Place acquir'd so much Learning as to distinguish them from English, pretended to an intimate Acquaintance with them."

Knowledge of the learned languages was the prime symbol of the superiority of the college educated, and Franklin was rankled by it. At Harvard commencements, Franklin continued, "Every Beetle-Scull seem'd well satisfy'd with his own Portion of Learning, tho' perhaps he was e'en just as ignorant as ever."[108] At sixteen, Franklin was cynical about the preferment that riches brought to those without ability; cynical about the clergy, too many of whom were in it for a good living; cynical about the pretensions of higher education.[109]

The next year, 1723, Franklin fled Boston and the domination of his older brother James, "hitchhiking," one may put it, to Philadelphia, and a year later, in November 1724, when he was eighteen, he ventured to London, where he found

---

[106] It is one small irony in the Franklin–Logan relationship that Logan for years aspired to gaining international recognition as a botanist, corresponded with Linnaeus, and published in the field in European journals. But he was never celebrated as a scientist. Franklin had a similar aspiration and in his forties became renowned in Europe for his discoveries relating to electricity, a subject in which Logan was also interested. Logan did not begrudge him that fame. If there was a rivalry, it was amicable.

[107] *The Papers of Benjamin Franklin*, ed. Leonard Labaree and Whitfield J. Bell, Jr. (New Haven, CT, 1959), I, 15.

[108] Ibid.

[109] Lemay, *Life of Benjamin Franklin* (2006), vol. I, 50, comments: "Franklin's frustration must have been overwhelming. His enormous self-discipline and ferocious private course of study may owe much to his father's decision to take him out of school."

work in the printing shop of Samuel Palmer. There a decisive and complicated awakening occurred when he was assigned randomly to set type for the third edition of William Wollaston's *Religion of Nature Delineated*, destined to be one of the two or three most widely read works of moral philosophy in the second quarter of the century. By 1760, nine editions of Wollaston had appeared. Like Logan a few years later, Franklin was piqued by Wollaston enough to attempt his own philosophical work, his *Dissertation on Liberty and Necessity, Pleasure and Pain*, a peculiar 35-page pamphlet that in 1725 he typeset and printed privately in an edition of a hundred copies.[110] In a couple of dozen pages Franklin denied the reality of evil and the existence of injustice, denied free will and human moral responsibility, and denied the existence of an afterlife with rewards and punishments. In elaborate reasoning, he also denied the personal immortality of the soul. Even if one were to interpret the entire pamphlet as a mere joke or persiflage (which is not impossible), such a performance is informative about Franklin's state of mind in 1725. The pamphlet expressed virtually total disaffection with not only the New England religious tradition but also with the Christian tradition in general, a perilous state of mind for a young man in that era.

A great deal of nonsense has been written over the years about this pamphlet by Franklin, but it is a work that does not deserve serious consideration outside of the sole context of Franklin's personal development—psychological, intellectual, and moral. Like the college disputations of Franklin's time or debating society propositions today, the arguments are a form of mental training not intended for exposure to public criticism. Franklin printed one hundred copies, but he later burned nearly all of them, presumably out of embarrassment. Typical of the genre, Franklin followed a chain of reasoning to the point of absurdity. The *Dissertation* was a half-facetious demonstration in which Franklin proved to himself that he, too, could write like a college-trained "philosopher," whatever the content.[111] I will come back to it in some detail.

---

[110] The first edition of the *Religion of Nature* was printed privately by the author. Before his death in 1724, Wollaston oversaw a second edition that, like the third (which Franklin worked on), was printed by Palmer. John Clarke of Hull published in 1725 *An Examination of the Notion of Moral Good and Evil, Advanced in a Late Book, entitled The Religion of Nature Delineated*, which was a reply to Wollaston, and before the year was out, there was already in print a *Defence of Mr. Wollaston's Notion of Moral Good and Evil* by an anonymous author who rebutted Clarke. Neither of these short books (they are really more like pamphlets) contains any indication of knowledge of Franklin's *Dissertation*, which, in any case, was of broader scope. The 1724 edition of Wollaston, Clarke's attack, and the anonymous defense, have all been reprinted in facsimile in a single volume, introduced by Stanley Tweyman, published by Scholar's Facsimiles & Reprints (Delmar, NY, 1974). On the popularity of Wollaston among the educated, see Fiering, *Jonathan Edwards's Moral Thought*, 132–35. *The Religion of Nature Delineated* was used as a text at Yale beginning in the 1740s at the latest. Samuel Johnson recommended it to Franklin for use at the new College of Philadelphia.

[111] This fact makes incomprehensible Perry Miller's comment in *The New England Mind: From Colony to Province*, 420, that Franklin was "so repelled [by Wollaston's *Religion of Nature*] that he attempted to answer it *drawing upon standard New England ideology.* . . ." (my italics). Carl Van Doren's comment about the *Dissertation* in *Benjamin Franklin* (New York, 1938), 52, is more apt: Franklin "was a young Bostonian trying to find reasons to do as he liked in London."

James Logan first read Wollaston's *Religion of Nature* in 1726, judging from a letter he wrote to William Burnet, Governor of New York, on November 7th of that year: "To my very great pleasure, I have lately seen the Religion of Nature Delineated, a piece for which one may justly, I hope, congratulate the age. Both the man, and the work appear equally wonderfull to me, the latter for its own excellency, and the first that a person of such great abilities, such vast strength of thought and erudition, should so long lie obscurely concealed in such a nation."[112] The *Religion of Nature* became Logan's inspiration for his own treatise on moral philosophy, as I noted earlier. Writing to Peter Collinson in November 1734, Logan related that he believed that he personally had deeper insights into the subject than anyone else he had read, and that it "appeared" to him "it were a pity" if his knowledge "should be quite lost, for were it but tolerably delineated, as Wollaston calls it, others more capable might possibly afterwards take it up and carry it to just length."[113]

It would be hard to imagine two more divergent responses to Wollaston, written at about the same time, than Franklin's at age nineteen and Logan's at age fifty-two. Logan was established in life with most fundamental personal issues resolved. His "Duties of Man" was an extended whole-hearted effort at making a contribution to the greatest philosophical debate of his time. Franklin had not yet defined himself, and his *Dissertation* was no more than a written exercise in self-discovery, a kind of life experiment, this time under a persona different than Mrs. Silence Dogood: that of the skeptical academic philosopher. His ultimate destruction of the book before he left London after an eighteen-month sojourn there signified not only that the direction of his life was not to be that of the Grub Street provocateur, but that by a kind of catharsis he had resolved whatever longing remained for a Harvard education.[114] This decisive act was a turning point in Franklin's life. It represented a decision to abandon the role of skeptic and satirist of the establishment, which he had cultivated since his youth, and to join society as at least a nominal conformer to the conventional English Christian values of the time. The printing of the *Dissertation* had brought Franklin an invitation to meet one of the lions of the London freethought coterie, Bernard Mandeville, author of the brilliant *Fable of the Bees* (1705, 1714), but Franklin had experienced enough of this group to recoil from their radicalism. The self-made tradesman dedicated to public service was a greater badge of honor.[115]

Franklin tells us in his *Autobiography* that the *Dissertation* was a direct response to Wollaston—"Some of his Reasonings not appearing to be well-founded" —but the pamphlet has only partly to do with Wollaston's thinking and was more

---

[112] Quoted in Wolf, ed. *Logan's Library*, 525.

[113] Most of Logan's letters to Collinson between 1736 and 1741 were transcribed by Edwin Wolf 2nd, who generously granted me permission to use his typescripts. Logan's Letterbooks A, B, and C, from which these transcripts come, are the property of the Historical Society of Pennsylvania. Logan's letter to Collinson of Nov. 14, 1734, is quoted in Wolf, ed., *Logan's Library*, 526.

[114] Only four original copies of Franklin's *Dissertation* have survived, at least one of which Franklin brought back with him to Philadelphia.

[115] Franklin relates in his *Autobiography* that on his last visit to Boston before his move to London, his father had warned him against "lampooning and libeling to which he thought I had too much inclination."

ambitious than a mere critique of Wollaston would have required. The *Religion of Nature* is the only book directly cited in the text of the *Dissertation*; it is clear, however, that Franklin had read Locke on motivation and was also versed in the literature of philosophical libertinism and skepticism, views that he had picked up, no doubt, after arriving in London. Indeed, insignificant as it was as a considered mature statement, Franklin's *Dissertation* was surely the most radical piece of freethought expounded by any American in the first half of the eighteenth century. The work is so extreme in its conclusions that one could make a case it was intended as satire, another piece of revenge against the academy, admission to which his father had denied him.[116] Yet, not surprisingly, only a few years after Franklin had attempted to subvert Wollaston's *Religion of Nature*, he himself had come to believe—or at least reconciled himself with—many of Wollaston's principles.

The basic argument of the *Dissertation* is that God in his "goodness" governs the entire creation in all its detail, that there can be no true moral freedom in such an iron-bound universe, and that there is no real distinction either in nature or from God between good and evil, virtue and vice. God is hardly essential to this argument, for Franklin in effect maintained in this early piece a naturalistic determinism or fatalism that requires God only as a First Mover.

The work has two parts: the first is metaphysical, the second empirical. The metaphysical section, by a series of deductions from first principles, sets up an age-old antinomy. If God is all-powerful, he must be responsible for all occurrences, including those "Things and Actions to which we give the Name of Evil, . . . [such] as Pain, Sickness, Want, Theft, Murder, &c." If He is all-good, He cannot be the cause of such evils (pp. 59–60). It appears, therefore, that it is necessary to choose between God's omnipotence and His benevolence, for He cannot have both attributes.

Franklin solved this dilemma by arguing that evil does not exist. Since God is all-powerful, he wrote, "there can be nothing either existing or acting in the Universe against or without his Consent; and what He consents to must be good, because He is good; therefore Evil doth not exist." Pain, sickness, want, and so on, "are not in reality Evils, Ills, or Defects in the Order of the Universe" (pp. 59–60). He also disposed easily of the scholastic distinction between what God positively does and what He permits to be done, which Wollaston had drawn upon as a way out from the dilemma between divine omnipotence and the existence of evil. Whatever the logical weaknesses of this traditional distinction between God's permission or allowance and His positive action, the distinction was in conformity with the theological principle that God is not completely knowable, that there is a mystery at the heart of things. Franklin's God, however, is a completely knowable metaphysical premise, the God of the philosophers, reduced to clarity and distinctness.

Not only is all that exists and occurs good, with evil merely an appearance, but it follows from the initial premises that all human actions are completely determined and necessarily "good." The creature receives all its power from God, Franklin wrote, "with which power the creature can do nothing contrary to the will

---

[116] Albert H. Smyth, who edited Franklin's writings in 1905, deliberately excluded the *Dissertation* from his ten-volume edition because, he said, the "work has no value, and it would be an injury and offence to the memory of Franklin to republish it."

of God, because God is almighty." What is not contrary to the will of God must be agreeable to it, and therefore must be good, because God is good. "A creature can do nothing but what is good" (p. 60). "Men will call actions by their fellow-creatures evil, but no one can act in such a way that it will be in itself really ill, or displeasing to God." As Alexander Pope asked provocatively a few years later, "If plagues or earthquakes break not Heav'n's design, / Why then a Borgia, or a Catiline?" Judgments of moral good and evil become, then, merely social conventions. There is no theological or transcendent basis for humanly ascribed values. Franklin at this point was verging on nihilism.

Wollaston had written: "But let us return to that, which is our main subject, the distinction between moral good and evil. Some have been so wild as to deny there is any such thing: but from what has been said here, it is manifest, that there is as certainly moral good and evil as there is true and false; and that there is a as natural and immutable a difference between those as between these, the difference at bottom being indeed the same." The prevalence of real evil in this world was proof, in Wollaston's view, of the necessity of an afterlife where God administered final justice. Leslie Stephen remarked in his great study of eighteenth-century British thought that Wollaston and Bishop Butler were almost alone in the first half of the eighteenth century in their willingness to face squarely the true existence of evil.[117]

Franklin's direct refutation of Wollaston's peculiar ethical theory, which had made the distinction between good and evil exactly equivalent to the distinction between truth and falsehood, came in here. According to Wollaston, the presence of good and evil is intrinsic to the universe and as much a part of its rational order as truth and falsehood, intelligible to man and in some fashion ordained by God. By Wollaston's reasoning, Franklin said, every action which is done according to truth is good, and every action contrary to truth is evil. "Thus if A steals a horse from B, and rides away upon him, he uses him not as what he is in truth, viz. the property of another, but as his own, which is contrary to truth, and therefore evil." In other words, just as all men are capable of making a distinction between truth and falsehood, so they also have an inbred faculty for distinguishing virtue and vice. The problem with Wollaston's position here is that truth logic has no content of itself. It is a formal, abstract system that is applicable to any set of objects for determining agreement or disagreement, or determining other relations, as in mathematics. In the example of the horse thief, Wollaston unwittingly supplied the moral content of the equation.

Franklin grasped this perfectly. Wollaston himself has said, Franklin observed, that "In order to judge rightly what any thing is, it must be considered, not only what it is in one respect, but also what it may be in any other respect . . . and the whole description of the thing ought to be taken in." Using this proposition of Wollaston's as authorization, Franklin went on to argue: "So in this case it ought to be consider'd, that A is naturally a covetous being, feeling an uneasiness in the want of B's Horse, which produces an Inclination for stealing him, stronger than his fear of punishment for so doing. This is truth likewise, and A acts according to it

---

[117] Stephen, *History of English Thought in the Eighteenth Century* (orig. publ. London, 1876; New York, 1962), vol. I, 112.

when he steals the horse" (p. 61). In other words, there can be many "true" descriptions of any event looked at from different angles, and the criterion of truth cannot of itself determine what elements are relevant to a specifically moral judgment as distinguished from a judgment about any other aspect of the same event.

Franklin's answer to Wollaston was, of course, not intended to justify or encourage theft. His rebuttal was "only for the sake of argument," he said, and will "certainly have no ill effect." Just as in the famous story of Zeno's slave, who when caught committing a theft pleaded to the Stoic sage that it was his necessitated fate to steal, to which his master answered without departing from his principles that it is also fated the slave was to be whipped for the crime; so Franklin concluded his analysis of Wollaston with the comment: "The order and course of things will not be affected by reasoning of this kind," for "'tis as just and necessary, and as much according to truth, for B to dislike and punish the theft of his horse, as it is for A to steal him."

Franklin's espousal of cosmological determinism based on the absolute extension of God's laws into His creation, such that there is no distinction between Creator and created in terms of governing principles, stamped him as a Spinozist, with God Himself absorbed into the universal system. Orthodox Calvinist determinists, such as Jonathan Edwards, also curtailed human freedom but emphasized God's unconditioned being outside of nature and His providential intervention into history via the Holy Spirit. In the religious tradition, the universe can never be wholly predictable.

The Hutchesonians were also implicit determinists in most of their arguments because, like Franklin, they believed in an ordered or providential universe, wherein actions were not left entirely to the accidents of free choice. But unlike Franklin, they were certain that virtue and vice are not simply illusory and matters of human invention. They believed in real defections from divine law, attributable to ignorance, perversity, corruption, ill-training, and so forth. The devil was not talked about, but he was there. A theologian or a philosopher who hoped to retain any ties at all to the Judaeo-Christian religious tradition had to believe that a benevolent God has somehow deliberately limited His own power, allowing room for real good and evil on earth, or, in other words, had to believe that there was not complete uniformity between God and nature in their operations. God remains outside of and greater than His creation. Spinoza was the supreme example of the heretical opposition to this truth, but similar ideas may be found not infrequently before him and independently of him afterwards.

Franklin capped the Spinozist first section of his *Dissertation* with the inevitable conclusion: "If there is no such thing as Free-will in creatures, there can be neither merit nor demerit in creatures." And, therefore, "Every creature must be equally esteem'd by the Creator." The assumption that in a truly determinist system there can be no merit or demerit was almost universal opinion, but it had been rarely examined closely until Jonathan Edwards, at mid-century, directly undertook to refute it. In Franklin's pamphlet the idea of liberty or free will is so sketchily developed that it is impossible even to tell what kind of determinism he had in mind that would be incompatible with individual moral responsibility. He pointed out that men might be said to have liberty when they are free from active opposition or coaction. "But it is a liberty of the same nature with the fall of a heavy body to the ground; it has liberty to fall, that is, it meets with nothing to hinder its fall, but at the same time it is necessitated to fall, and has no power or liberty to remain suspended" (p. 62). The comparison to gravity suggests physical determinism that might indeed be inconsistent with moral responsibility, as though a person were under the influence of a drug that impels him this way or that, in short, an external agent. But men are also motivated by mental phenomena that they accept as their own, identify with, and willingly take personal responsibility for, at least at the moment of decision. Such motives or, better, reasons, we treat as being an expression of some aspect of ourselves. In this sense, acts may be determined and are yet praiseworthy or damnable. As many theologians had pointed out prior to Franklin, God or Jesus Christ cannot do evil; they are necessarily good, yet they are considered praiseworthy.[118]

The second section of Franklin's *Dissertation* was designed to reinforce by means of psychological evidence the argument of the first part, that virtue and vice are illusory, and beyond that to show that all people are equally happy (or unhappy) in this world, making life on earth perfectly just. There is no special divine reward and punishment on earth, nor is there a need for an afterlife in order to rectify the alleged injustices in this world, since "all the Works of the Creator are equally esteem'd by Him," and they are, "as in Justice they ought to be, equally us'd" (p. 63).

Franklin's starting point was probably some remarks in Locke's *Essay Concerning Human Understanding* that adumbrated a universal theory of motivation based on the avoidance of pain. There were suggestions of this kind of thinking prior to Locke in various of the egoist theories that attempted to expose the non-rational bases of conduct, but usually the desire for pleasure was cited along with avoidance of pain as a primary motive. Locke maintained, however, that "the chief, if not only spur to human industry and action is uneasiness. For whatsoever good is proposed, if its absence carries no displeasure or pain with it, if a man be easy and content without it, there is no desire of it, nor endeavour after it; there is no more but a bare velleity, the term used to signify the lowest degree of desire . . . when there is so little uneasiness in the absence of anything, that it carries a man no further than some faint wishes for it, without any more effectual or vigorous use of the means to attain it."[119]

Franklin elevated these few words into an extraordinary conception of pain as the fundamental principle of life. Pain, he said, is what "distinguishes Life and Consciousness from unactive unconscious Matter. To know or be sensible of Suffering or being acted upon is to live" (p. 63). Such remarks had typically been made about the passions in general, which were seen as the energy of living activity. Franklin seems to have assumed that a passion of any kind, indeed a stimulus of any kind, is painful by definition. Pain and uneasiness, he said, is caused by something outside of and distinct from "the Mind itself." "The Soul must first be acted upon before it

---

[118] The question was common in college disputations. Yale College theses in 1735 and 1738 affirmed both divine government and human freedom: 1735, "Praescientia divina non tollit libertatem humanam" (Divine foreknowledge does not eliminate human freedom); 1738, "Moralis necessitas non destruit libertatum naturalem" (Moral necessity does not destroy natural freedom). There were similar topics at Harvard commencements, which were public events in Boston and Cambridge in Franklin's youth, and he would have been aware of the disputations.

[119] Locke, *Essay*, Bk. II, xx, 6.

can re-act." The newborn infant has no consciousness of its own existence until it has received its first "Sensation of Pain; then, and not before, it begins to feel itself, is rous'd and put into Action; then it discovers its Powers and Faculties, and exerts them to expel the Uneasiness" (p. 64). Thus, Franklin wrote, "we are first mov'd by Pain, and the whole succeeding Course of our Lives is but one continu'd Series of Action with a View to be freed from it" (p. 64).

Franklin waxed grandiloquent on how "necessary a Thing in the Order and Design of the Universe this Pain or Uneasiness is, and how beautiful in its Place!" One cannot be sure here that he is not parodying Shaftesbury, who saw beauty and order in just about everything. If pain were banished from the world, "all the Animal Creation would immediately stand stock still, exactly in the Posture they were in the Moment Uneasiness departed; not a Limb, not a Finger would henceforth move; we should all be reduc'd to the Condition of Statues, dull and unactive. . . . Tis impossible to assign any other Cause for the Voluntary Motion of an Animal than its uneasiness in Rest. What a different Appearance then would the Face of Nature make, without it! How necessary is it! And how unlikely that the Inhabitants of the World ever were, or that the Creator ever design'd they should be, exempt from it." Franklin's paean to pain is surely one of the crowning moments of nonsense in the history of cosmic perfectionism and monism. Thirty years later this bubble was burst when Hume listed among the proofs that God is not altogether benevolent the frequency with which nature uses pain as a motivating factor. If the Creator had been truly benevolent, pleasure would be the only stimulus.[120]

From this unlikely psychological principle, which like the amoralism of the first part of the *Dissertation* defied common experience, Franklin moved to an even more eccentric proposition. Since uneasiness is "the first Spring and Cause of all Action," it must be the source of all desire. The desire, then, is "equal" to the uneasiness. The exact nature of the measureable quantities here was, of course, left vague, and no distinction was made between a desire, which can exist even with a surfeit, and a need, which springs from deprivation or indigence. The fulfillment of the desire, Franklin continued, produces a sensation of pleasure exactly proportionate to the desire. "Pleasure is that Satisfaction which arises in the Mind upon, and is caus'd by, the accomplishment of our Desires" (p. 65). Now since uneasiness is the direct cause of desire, and quantitatively proportionate to it; and since the fulfillment or satisfaction of desire is the basis of all pleasure whatsoever, with the quantity of the pleasure exactly proportionate to the desire, it follows that pain is the cause of the pleasure, and that pain and pleasure are always exactly equivalent in value. "Pleasure and Pain are in their Nature inseparable: So Many Degrees as one Scale of the Ballance descends, so many exactly the other ascends; and one cannot rise or fall without the Fall or Rise of the other: 'Tis impossible to taste of Pleasure, without feeling its preceding proportionate Pain; or to be sensible of Pain, without having its necessary Consequent Pleasure" (p. 66).

---

[120] Cf. David Hume, *Dialogues Concerning Natural Religion*, ed. Norman Kemp Smith (Indianapolis, IN: Prentice Hall, 1947), 205–206. Arguing against the assumed goodness of the Creator, Hume considered it neither "necessary nor unavoidable" that "pains, as well as pleasures, are employed to excite all creatures to action. . . . Pleasure alone, in its various degrees, seems to human understanding sufficient for the purpose."

Franklin referred to no authorities for this theory, and so far as I have discovered it was not held strictly by any moderns, although there may be some Classical antecedents. Malebranche, who was perhaps the leading theorist of the passions at the turn of the century, asserted that "Pain is a real and true Evil," and it "is no more the privation of pleasure, than pleasure is the privation of pain; for there is a difference between not feeling pleasure, or being deprived of the sensation of it, and actually suffering pain."[121] Locke had pointed out the obvious truth that "the removal or lessening of a pain is considered, and operates, as a pleasure: and the loss or diminishing of a pleasure, as a pain." But this psychological fact implies no metaphysical balance in the universe, nor does it assume that all pleasures and pains are rooted in each other.

It is obvious that Franklin adhered to this fragile theory only to back up his more general arguments. First, it followed from this theory, according to Franklin, that there can be no disinterested action, and therefore, no merit or demerit. This proposition corresponded to his earlier conclusion: "How can any Action be meritorious of Praise or Dispraise, Reward or Punishment, when the natural Principle of Self-Love is the only and irresistible Motive to it?" (p. 65). Self-love here meant for Franklin acting out of regard for one's personal pleasure or pain. Technically, such forms of self-love are not necessarily incompatible with virtue—one may, for example, derive personal pleasure from charitable deeds—but Franklin was taking what F. B. Kaye has called the "rigorist" position.[122]

Secondly, if all pleasure and pain is reciprocal, then "no Condition of Life or Being is in itself better or preferable to another: The Monarch is not more happy than the Slave, nor the Beggar more miserable than Croesus" (pp. 66–67). It followed from this proposition that there is no need for an afterlife to compensate for the "suppos'd Inequality of Pain and Pleasure" in the present existence. "Pain naturally and infallibly produces a Pleasure in proportion to it"; therefore, "every individual Creature, in any State of Life, have an equal Quantity of each, so that there is not, on that Account, any Occasion for a future Adjustment" (p. 66). There are other radical ideas in Franklin's *Dissertation*, but enough has been recounted here to convey the silly flavor of the work and contrast it to Logan's serious thinking.

A single contemporary assessment of Franklin's *Dissertation* has survived, a mere fragment, but it is the only response that I know of, and it is by an American—none other than James Logan, whose unpublished manuscripts contain a few words about Franklin's scandalous little book. The fragment was written in about 1736, and we can only guess at the circumstances. Probably when Franklin learned that Logan was working on the problem of the will, which was the topic of the sixth chapter of his never-published ethics treatise, he impishly passed on to him a copy of the *Dissertation*, which was, of course, printed anonymously. Franklin almost certainly never let Logan know that he was the author, and he then enjoyed

---

[121] *Search After Truth*, Sault trans., Bk. 5, chap. 3, p. 16.

[122] Bernard Mandeville, *Fable of the Bees*, ed. F. B. Kaye (Oxford, 1924). Kaye, in his illuminating introduction, observed that Mandeville deliberately defined virtue as conduct that is purely intellectual and disinterested in order to generalize about the prevalence of vice in the world. A later two-page essay of Franklin's on the theme "Men are Naturally Benevolent as Well as Selfish," (*Pennsylvania Gazette*, Nov. 30, 1732) is, in effect, a retraction of the rigorism in his *Dissertation*.

the burlesque of hearing Logan's denunciations of the heretical 1725 pamphlet as though the author was an utter stranger. The fragment from Logan reads as follows:

> [?]. . . had directly ensued in a little Pamphlet published in the year 1725, sent as its Author pretends to his friend[123] [along] with Wollastons Religion of nature delineated wherein the Reasonableness of a belief of the Immortality of the Soul being asserted from the inequality of the Distribution of the Goods of this Life and of Pleasure and Pain; in order to overthrow an Opinion so dangerous to the Atheistical tenets that writer and probably his friends had embraced[,] he there with great resolution undertakes to raise a superstructure on the foundation of that Chapter of Lock which we may rationally believe was very far from that great Man 's intention, to prove that the Degrees of Pleasure and Pain are exactly equal to every Individual in this life, and therefore that there can be no occasion for any further adjustment or compensation to those who suffer for the cause of virtue and that in the truth of things in regard to the Supreme Being there can be no such thing as virtue and vice in the world and his whole argumentation turns on this[,] that all Action whatever springs from Pain or uneasiness, that without it all the animal kind would stand as he says stock still without action or Motion, that Pain produces a Desire to be freed from it exactly equal in Degree to the Pain, that all Pleasure is founded in the gratification of Desire[,] which Pleasure and Desire are also in degree always exactly equal.[124]

No subsequent work of Franklin's was ever again as "academic" or irresponsible as the *Dissertation*. In about 1746 Franklin wrote to his philosophically-minded friend in New York, Cadwallader Colden: It is only "with Reluctance" I engage in metaphysics. "The great Uncertainty I have found in that Science; the wide Contradictions and endless Disputes it affords; and the horrible Errors I led myself into when a young Man, by drawing a Chain of plain Consequences as I thought them, from true Principles, have given me a Disgust to what I was once extreamly fond of."[125] In his autobiography Franklin referred to the *Dissertation* as "another Erratum" in the book of his life. Within three years of his return to Philadelphia from London, Franklin had greatly modified the tenor of his earlier speculations.[126]

There is another documented reciprocity between James Logan and Benjamin Franklin specifically in the area of moral thought (they cooperated on a number of other matters outside of that particular realm, as we know). As Logan labored over his "Duties of Man," he sent portions of it, we have seen, to his Quaker friend

---

[123] Franklin's *Dissertation* is prefaced with a letter to "Mr. J. R.," identified in Labaree and Bell, eds., *Papers*, as Franklin's actual friend James Ralph.

[124] From the Logan-Alverthorpe MSS, Historical Society of Pennsylvania, fragment included in Logan's sketch for chap. 6 of the "Duties of Man."

[125] *Papers*, III, 88–89. The date of this letter is probable, and Colden was not the original recipient, but Franklin sent Colden a copy of it. The original correspondent is unknown.

[126] The major indication of this change is the private religious service that Franklin formulated in 1728, entitled "Articles of Belief and Acts of Religion." In it, he prays that he "may be preserved from Atheism and Infidelity, Impiety and Profaneness . . . Irreverence and Ostentation. . . ."

in London, Peter Collinson, asking Collinson to put them into the hands of knowledgeable English friends for comment. Logan did not, however, share his work in progress with anyone in America it would appear, with a single exception— Franklin. Thus, just as Logan was the only American to have read Franklin's *Dissertation*, although without knowing the true author, so Franklin was probably the only contemporary American to have read any part of Logan's never published "Duties of Man."

J. A. Leo Lemay records in his wonderfully meticulous unfinished multivolume biography of Franklin that in 1736 or 1737 Logan asked Franklin "to read and criticize" a portion of the "Duties of Man." Franklin responded:

> Having read the Chapter on Moral Good or Virtue, with all the Attention I am Capable of, amidst the many little Cares that Continually infest me, I shall, as the Author Condescends to desire, give my Opinion of it, and that with all Sincerity and Freedom, neither apprehending the Imputation of Flattery on the one hand, nor that of Ill Manners on the other.

It is obvious from this careful beginning how much Franklin feared damaging his relationship with Logan with a harsh judgment. Continuing, Franklin wrote to Logan:

> I think the Design excellent—and the Management of it in the Main, good; a short Summary of the Chapter plac'd at the Beginning, and little Summaries of each Paragraph in the Margin being only necessary, and what will in my opinion sufficiently remove any Disgust that the Authors dilate Manner of Writing may give to some Readers; And the whole is so curious and entertaining, that I know not where any thing can be spared. It seems to me,

Franklin continued,

> that the Author is a little too severe upon Hobbes, whose Notion, I imagine, is somewhat nearer the Truth than that which makes the State of Nature a State of Love: But the Truth perhaps lies between both Extreams. I think what is said upon Musick, might be enlarged to Advantage by showing that what principally makes a Tune agreeable, is the Conformity between its Air or Genius, and some Motion, Passion or Affection of the Mind, which the Tune imitates.

Franklin then went on to make a suggestion that later he himself introduced in his own work on the means of becoming virtuous:[127]

> I should have been glad to have the Virtues enumerated, distinguish'd, and the proper Ideas affix'd to each Name; which I have not yet seen scarce two Authors agreeing therein, some annexing more, others fewer and different ideas to the Same Name. But I think there is some Incorrectness of Sentiment in what the Author has said of Temperance concerning which I have not the time to explain myself in writing.[128]

---

[127] Fiering, "Benjamin Franklin and the Way to Virtue," *American Quarterly*.
[128] *Papers*, 2:184–85.

It is easy to imagine the issue of the proper definition of temperance coming up in Franklin's next face-to-face talk with Logan.

A couple of other small works by Franklin deserve a quick mention in relation to his conversations with Logan on moral philosophy. On November 30, 1732, Franklin published a very brief essay in the *Pennsylvania Gazette*, his newspaper, under the pseudonym "Y.Z.": "Men are Naturally Benevolent as Well as Selfish." And in February 1735, also in the *Gazette*, he published an essay, again under a pseudonym: "Self-Denial Is Not the Essence of Virtue." Although there is no direct mention of Logan in either case, it seems likely that these pieces, given their timing, addressed central questions he was in the midst of discussing with his Quaker friend. It was in this period, too, that Franklin printed for Logan his *Latter Part of the Charge to the Grand Inquest, September 24, 1733*, and when Logan retired as a judge, Franklin printed a few years later his farewell to the law, *The Charge Delivered . . . to the Grand Inquest . . . April 13, 1736*. The latter, as I have noted, was a distillation of some of Logan's conclusions in "The Duties of Man Deduced from Nature."

To conclude, beyond Franklin there were a handful of people in colonial America who might have been astute and sympathetic readers of Logan's manuscript, but only a handful. The greatest of moral philosophers on these shores was Jonathan Edwards, who would have understood Logan well but who would also have been adamantly opposed to Logan's basic premise that the foundations of true virtue could be revealed by attendance to the voice of "nature." Edwards's works covered the same ground as Logan's manuscript—passions, will, reason, and so forth—but with far more acumen and depth. For Logan, William Wollaston, Francis Hutcheson, and others were influences; for Edwards they were contenders to whom he was intellectually equal and whose false reasoning in his eyes had to be refuted. Samuel Johnson of Connecticut, who in 1754 was invited to become the first president of King's College in New York (later Columbia University) and who published at length on issues relating to moral philosophy, would have been an astute and informed reader, but the two men did not know each other, although Franklin knew both and recruited Johnson to help with his plan to found a college in Philadelphia.[129]

---

[129] Norman Fiering, "President Samuel Johnson and the Circle of Knowledge," *William and Mary Quarterly*, XXVIII, No. 2 (April 1971).

# For Further Discussion

Belatedly, I came upon the online site of the Stenton house museum, James Logan's elegant home in Philadelphia, which is beautifully preserved thanks to the Colonial Dames (see www.stenton.org). The curator at the house, Laura C. Keim, is doing a marvelous job of recovering Logan's life at Stenton, not so much in his official governmental roles, or in his busy life as a merchant, or in his deep involvement in learned study, but as a homeowner, father, husband, and, alas, master. Logan not only employed indentured servants, he was also a slave owner, a practice that Quakers at the time increasingly eschewed.

I am inclined to mention this here because it is one more example of the strange anomaly that the institution of slavery was in various instances in colonial British America from the mid-eighteenth century forward. We are struck by the high-mindedness of figures like Thomas Jefferson and the seeming contradiction of his acceptance of slavery. Here we have Logan, assiduously pondering the fundamentals of morality, engaged in speculation on the constitution of virtue and what underlies it, while oblivious, it would seem, to the gross immorality of human bondage. What kind of intellectual disjuncture is this? Charges of mere hypocrisy are easy but miss the mark entirely.

There is no space to answer this question at length here, but a proper answer must take into account our complexity as humans: our typical blindness to what is customary or to what has for decades or centuries served our interests without full evaluation of the consequences; or our mental evasiveness when challenged on moral grounds that bring into question the whole structure of our lives; or the easy acceptance of what we simply inherit, that which we are born into and see as the norm, leaving aside financial interests. Where such blindness is the rule, when great crimes are hardly noticed because of their seeming normality, we have to be told emphatically that a reconciliation is needed, sometimes told repeatedly, until at last a new balance is established without contradiction. To this day, moral progress, humane progress, is made up of such steps.

# Index

## A
affections, social, 34ff
  as distinguished from passions,
    49–51
afterlife
  as moral reinforcement, 3
Ames, William
  and Harvard, 4
antinomianism, 3
approbativeness, 29–34. *See also*
    pride.
  as inducement to morality, 29
Aristotle, 2
attention, 44

## B
Balguy, John
  *Foundation of Moral Goodness,*
    57n, 60–64
beauty
  perception of as model, 58–59, 63
  universal standards of, 59
benevolence, 6–7, 11, 22, 29, 37, 58.
    *See also* benevolism
benevolence, universal
  and Cumberland, 6
benevolism, 7, 13, 56
Bible and moral philosophy, 2
Boyle, Robert
  and natural theology, 25
Browne, Peter, 22–23
  on Locke, 42–43
Butler, Bishop Joseph, 33, 51n
  *Fifteen Sermons,* 23

## C
*Charge . . . from the Bench to the
    Grand Inquest . . .*
  printed work by Logan, 17, 67

children
  moral capacity of, 34–35, 57
Christian ethics, 2
Christian revelation, 2
Clarke, Samuel, 5–7, 17, 22n, 57–61
Classical ethics
  as behavioral, 2
Collinson, Peter
  correspondent in London, 14
compassion
  Logan on, 35
conscience, 2–3. *See also* synteresis
  as a passion, 53
Cumberland, Richard, 5–8, 11–13,
    24–25, 50n, 57n

## D
deism
  in the 17th century, 3
Derham, William
  and natural theology, 25
Descartes, 5
  influence of, 13, 24, 48
divine design, 7

## E
Edwards, Jonathan
  as moral philosopher, 16, 21
ethics. *See also* moral philosophy.
  stages in history of, 4–5

## F
family, 22ff, 27
  as natural basis for expansive love,
    28–29
  natural affection within, 28
final causes, 38–39
fitness
  as moral category, 60–61

Exchange

NOV 2 1 2022